ALL IN A DAY'S WORK

ALL IN A DAY'S WORK

A wealth of witty
after-dinner anecdotes
from the famous

Edited by Mark Hornsby

PIATKUS

Copyright © 1989 stories collected by Mark Hornsby

First published in Great Britain in 1989 by
Judy Piatkus (Publishers) Ltd of
5 Windmill Street, London W1

British Library Cataloguing in Publication Data

All in a day's work.
  1. Humorous anecdotes in English, 1945 – Anthologies
  I. Hornsby, Mark
  8289'402'08

  ISBN 0-86188-877-4
  ISBN 0-86188-882-0 (pbk)

Cartoons by Paul Davies
Design by Ken Leeder

Phototypeset in 12/12pt Compugraphic Goudy O.S. by
Action Typesetting Limited, Gloucester
Printed and bound in Great Britain by
Mackays of Chatham plc

The royalties from this book will be donated to
Myalgic Encephalomyelitis (M.E.)

MYALGIC
ENCEPHALOMYELITIS

M.E., or post-viral syndrome, as the illness is sometimes known, is the disease process which occurs in a person who contracts an acute viral illness. M.E. can effect every part of the body, bringing pain and paralysis to the muscles. It also attacks the central nervous system, bringing exhaustion, intense malaise and inability to concentrate — to name only three of the many symptoms which can occur. In the early stages M.E. is characterised by the patient's inability to perform even the simplest of everyday tasks. M.E. patients can and do make a significant or a full recovery even after long periods of time, but as yet there is no drug that will cure the illness or significantly alter the course of the disease.

Royalties from the sale of this book will go towards research into the disease.

CONTRIBUTORS

Jimmy Hood 54
Roy Hudd 54
David Icke 55
John Inman 57
Gordon Jackson 57
David Jacobs 58
Sally Jones 59
John Junkin 60
Gorden Kaye 61
Chris Kelly 62
Kenneth Kendall 63
John Kettley 63
Roy Kinnear 64
The Krankies 65
Maureen Lipman 66
Barbara Lott 67
Ian McCaskill 68
Leo McKern 69
Norris McWhirter 70
Sally Magnusson 72
Alfred Marks 72
Patrick Moore 73
Mike Morris 74
Brian Murphy 74
Derek Nimmo 75
Tom O'Connor 78
Ian Ogilvy 79
Bill Owen 79
Nick Owen 80
Jeremy Paxman 81

Arthur Pentelow 81
Maggie Philbin 82
Frederick Pyne 82
Beryl Reid 83
Anneka Rice 83
Sue Robbie 84
Robert Robinson 85
Jean Rogers 85
Rev. Roger Royle 86
Andrew Sachs 86
Mike Scott 88
Brough Scott 88
Sir Harry Secombe 90
Dinah Sheridan 95
William G. Stewart 96
Alastair Stewart 96
Alan Titchmarsh 98
Barry Took 99
Carol Vorderman 99
Geoffrey Wheeler 100
June Whitfield 100
Roger Whittaker 101
Desmond Wilcox 103
Frank Williams 106
Simon Williams 107
Wincey Willis 108
Bob Wilson 110
Ernie Wise 110
Terry Wogan 111
Jimmy Young 111

JOSS ACKLAND
Actor

To celebrate our anniversary we decided to escape the family and fly to Amsterdam for a romantic weekend. That evening we took a boat on the canal, thinking what bliss to be alone together. As the boat slipped from its moorings a couple came to sit opposite us. Imagine our surprise to discover that they were our next-door neighbours!

JENNY AGUTTER
Actress

I was playing the part of the maid in *Breaking the Silence*, and during one scene with Gemma Jones, I had to clear the room and unpack some suitcases. At an appropriate moment in the scene, another actor enters. However, one night, thinking that he was late for his entrance (we heard him running round the stage) he burst through the door and announced, 'I am here!' We looked surprised as he had arrived 5 minutes too early. But, quickly redeeming the situation, he added, 'And I'll return in 5 minutes!'

THE LATE
EAMONN ANDREWS
C.B.E.

Chairman, Presenter, Interviewer

I can remember one of the early 'What's my Line?'
programmes where, as you know, the panel have to guess
the occupation of the challengers. I blew the whole show
in one second. A young man who was a waiter in the
Caprice restaurant in London, was all set to challenge the
panel and I introduced him and intended to say 'This man
is wage-earning' (the only sort of clue we are ever supposed
to give the panel) when, instead of which, I said, without
hearing myself saying it, of course, 'This man is a waiter!'
I couldn't understand why the panel and the audience fell
around laughing until I finally realised what I'd said.

FIONA ARMSTRONG
Newscaster

I have decided to tell you a couple of stories from my
broadcasting career. Like when I worked in local radio and
told the good citizens of Reading that it was 8:30 instead
of 7:30 in the morning. I'm sure there were a few thousand
listeners choking on their coffee that morning, thinking
that they were late for work! Or like saying in the weather
forecast that 'funny smells' were expected, instead of 'sunny
spells!' Or, in television, reading the news and suddenly
feeling the chair (which foolishly was on casters) sliding
away from me. Or reading the introduction to a piece of
film which doesn't appear − three tries! I know these
shouldn't really be funny, but looking back you have to
laugh!

GEORGE BAKER

Actor/Writer

Quite an amusing incident happened to me when I was
going to New Zealand to make four films from Ngaio Marsh
stories. My youngest daughter was then about seven and
not terribly happy about my going away. I arrived at
Heathrow and went through to the VIP lounge where I
waited for my flight to be called. I had already passed my
suitcases through and was only left with my hand luggage.
When my flight was called I went through the screening
barrier and customs. They opened my hand luggage and
there, to my horror and their amusement, was my
daughter's toy panda. She had sent her favourite toy with
me to keep me company. We all had a nice laugh about it
but, of course, I was left with the predicament of what to
do with it for the next six months. I decided to put on a
brave face and put it out at all the hotels I stayed at.
Sometimes the chamber maids would put it down on my
pillow when they made the beds.

You'll be glad to hear that I gave up cuddly toys the
moment I got back to England and was able to return the
panda to its rightful owner.

RICHARD BAKER

O.B.E., R.D.

Broadcaster

Television personalities are quite often recognised when they go around the country, and although this is generally a quite gratifying experience, it can occasionally be disconcerting. As a newsreader on BBC-TV for some 25 years, I received more than my share of TV exposure, so I was not surprised when a small boy came up to me outside the studios one day and asked for an autograph.

'Certainly.' I said. 'Do you know who I am?'

'No,' he replied bluntly. 'Who are you?'

'I'm a newsreader,' I said.

'Never mind,' answered the boy kindly, 'Newsreaders are good swaps!'

JOHNNY BALL

Writer/Presenter

MY FIRST AUDITION

Buying a drum kit for £20 when I was 16½ seemed a sensible move towards fufilling my long felt desire to be in 'show business', and I immediately threw my whole efforts into teaching myself, in the hope of reaching professional standard in a couple of years. I practised to a rigid timetable which demanded 24 hours per week in addition to my 44-hour daytime job. I felt I was getting on fine, but my only practical experience was a local hop, with a violin, piano and drums trio which was a fiasco, so I couldn't really assess my standard or rate of progress, and then I was called up to join the RAF.

This, I knew, was my big chance. If I was good enough to get into the band, I would be surrounded by real musicians and could learn from them. So, on my third day in the RAF I arrived at West Kirby in an ill-fitting uniform, and talked my way into the Bandmaster's office to find a wee Scottish Flight Sergeant whose whole life had been music.

'Och, not another drummer,' was his opening remark, and my heart sank in my new, stiff boots. 'Have ye ever played a side drum?' This was it, the crunch question. If I said 'No' there was a chance that I would be out without even touching a stick, but if I said 'Yes' I might immediately be found out in a lie.

'Er, no, but I'm sure I'll be able to,' I blurted out. 'Alright,' he said, 'put that drum on and let's see what you can do.'

I picked up a pair of drumsticks as thick as brush handles and then took up the side drum and slung it round my neck. I looked up to see the Sergeant and his Corporal and the other chap present, first smile and then crease up with laughter.

'Ye did say ye hadnae played one before?'
'Yes?'

'Och, it's just as well, yer supposed to put one arm through the strap.'

I looked down to realise that I had just looped the belt round my neck and the stupid drum hung down my around knees. Totally embarrassed, I threaded my arm through the strap.

'Alright laddy, give me a roll,' came the command.

Adjusting the unwieldy sticks in my sweaty hands, I struck up a roll, only to find that the drum, under the weight of the blows, disappeared behind my left leg. The noise of the roll stopped, to be replaced by the uncontrollable giggles of my examiners. I tried again with the same effect, and again. By now I was purple and the sweat ran down my face as I tried to control the uncontrollable drum. I felt utterly sick.

'Och, hang on laddy. Oh deary, deary me, we certainly do get 'em. Look Alec,' he said to his Corporal, 'hold the thing for him . . . right now laddy, have a go.'

This was it. The moment of truth. All the practice including the daily exercise of rolling for five minutes against the clock, would be in vain, unless . . . I rolled, and the sound steadied down, evened out and then rose to a crescendo of noise, broken only by the Flight Sergeant jumping to his feet and pointing and shouting.

'Yer in laddy. That's the best bloody drum roll I've heard in a long while.'

Half an hour later, I had shown myself capable of playing every piece of drum music in their repertoire, which was more a surprise to me than it was to them, and two weeks later out of a corps of sixteen drummers, I was chosen to play my first true musical engagement, the drummer behind a thirty-piece concert brass band to an audience of well over a thousand at the Liverpool Stadium. And the piece the Bandmaster chose to open the concert? 'Oklahoma' which begins with a solo drum roll, which starts quietly and then rises to a crescendo of noise.

JENI BARNETT
Actress/Writer/Presenter

Way back in the dim distant past when buses were buses and London wasn't one huge traffic jam, I was travelling on a bus from Putney to Camden.

The conductor was merrily whistling ... (You see what I mean about the dim distant past!) and I was staring contentedly out of the window. I always lounged on the three seats by the conductor, right in the thick of it, you understand.

By the time we got to Hammersmith several people had got on and got off, but more had got on than off so there was little room for anything, let alone lounging.

It was customary, then, for 'Gentlemen' to give up their seats to 'Ladies' and it was customary then, also, for young whipper-snappers like myself (I did say this was a historical piece!) to vacate their seats too. So there was much to-ing and fro-ing, and jumping up and sitting down and to cap it all it was raining. There was also the smell of steaming 'Pacamacs' and the inconvenience of two dozen soaking-wet cumbersome umbrellas.

Still the conductor whistled ... Margaret Thatcher hadn't been invented then so there was still something to whistle about.

However, by the time we got to Phoenix (Sorry I couldn't resist that) ... by the time we got to King's Cross the bus was jam-packed, choc-a-bloc, cram-full of heaving, saturated bodies, all wanting to alight at the next stop.

And it was into this scenario that up stood a frail, white-haired woman of around 86 years of age. She had the sweet smile of someone who is blissfully unaware of the misery of others, not because she was unkind, I hasten to add, but simply because she was 86 years of age ... and deaf! I knew she was deaf because I noticed her hearing-aid when she got on the bus.

She smiled and made her way to the right-hand front seat.

She smiled as the whistling conductor took her fare.

7

She smiled as the bus emptied and filled itself over and over again.

She smiled as she stood up to get off at St. Pancras; and holding her walking stick aloft so as not to inconvenience her fellow travellers, she made her way, patiently, through the packed bus.

When she came face to face with me on the three seater, she smiled harder, her arm aloft brandishing her walking stick like the Olympic Torch.

Being 86, remember, it was difficult for her to maintain this classical pose. As her arm crumpled she hung her walking stick on the wire bell cord.

The bell went, 'Ding!'

The bus stopped.

She hung on and the bell dung again.

The bus started.

She pulled.

It dung.

The bus stopped.

Ding.

Start.

Pull.

Ding.

Stop.

Start.

She was deaf remember.

Ding.

Stop.

Start.

We were being shunted back and fourth like Cuban rhumba dancers. And so it went on with her totally oblivious of the chaos she was causing.

The conductor stopped whistling, *thank God*, and I started laughing.

The person next to me started laughing.

And opposite, and next to them, until the whole downstairs of the bus was screaming, and writhing with hysteria.

I laughed so much I missed my stop.

The conductor finally managed to stop the bus, get out,

and explain to the driver who it was that was 'Playing silly beggers.'

'Our Lady of the Cane', still ignorant of her part in the pantomime, alighted at St. Pancras and walked off, her face in an angelic grin.

THELMA BARLOW

Mavis in Coronation Street

I was travelling by car to collect a friend whose car had broken down. My own vehicle wouldn't go faster than 30 miles an hour and I feared that I might need rescuing myself, but we managed to get home eventually. It was only when I took my car to the garage the next day that we found the problem. A very large peppermint had got stuck behind the accelerator pedal, a 30-mile limit was imposed — or do I mean limint?

HONOR BLACKMAN

Actress

One of the funniest interviews I have ever had was during my promotion tour for *Goldfinger*. For some reason my lovely publicity man, Tom Carlyle, and I got to Birmingham somewhat late and we went into the TV studio only two or three minutes before my interview was due. The young interviewer inquired as to what questions I would like to be asked. I said that he could ask me anything; indeed I preferred not to know what was coming. This seemed to make him doubly nervous when I had intended that it should make life easier for him.

I was wearing the gold finger which had been made by some glamorous jeweller from a mould of my finger. The director instructed us as to the fact that he would open the interview on a close-up of this finger, then pull back to include the whole of me, waist up, at which point the interviewer was to speak.

They started the countdown, ten, nine, eight ... At every count the interviewer, head down, locked his hands tighter and intoned 'God ..., Christ ...,' and worse. My heart went out to him but there was nothing I could do. The camera was on my finger, it began slowly tracking back, but he spoke straight off and I was introduced before I was seen. I sat there smiling, hoping that I looked relaxed with that stupid little finger stuck in the air (two security men stayed within feet of me all the time I wore it); there was an agonising pause and then the interviewer wrenched out a question.

'Tell me, Miss Blackman, what is it like being half male and half female?'

I laughed so much that I thought I would never get an answer out. Finally since I was wearing a very low-cut dress I bent forward and said, 'Which half did you have in mind for which?'

Having told this story, I realise that those who have never seen my 'Avengers' with the judo and the black leather and who possibly have not seen *Goldfinger* (are there some?) when I threw Sean in the hay may wonder what possessed our nervous interviewer to articulate such a question.

I have felt, ever since, that I can no longer be surprised by a question — but I *had* said that I preferred not to know what was coming!

ISLA BLAIR

Actress

I was on my way to pick up my mother from Victoria station when I realised I was early and decided to take the scenic route through Belgravia. I saw what looked like a newly open dress shop, white paint, blue and white striped awning and two pots of geraniums either side of the door. In the window was one pale cream silk dress looking expensive and inviting. I parked the car and went in. The interior of the shop looked as exclusive as the exterior and smelt French — the air was heavy with Gauloises and Pierre Balmain perfume. There were one or two dresses hanging on the rail in polythene bags and I recognised the Jean Muir and Jasper Conran models along with the Bruce Oldfields and Edwina Ronays. Realising that this was way outside the budget of my dreams I moved away from the rail of dresses I had been thumbing through, when a very smart lady appeared carrying a bowl of white roses.

'Yes madam, may I help you?'

'Oh, no thank you, I'm just having a look about if I may.' I replied.

There was a very long pause.

'Madam, this is a dry cleaners.'

RABBI LIONEL BLUE
Broadcaster/Writer

My mother has always been an intrepid woman, who would try her hand at anything, and indeed lend her hand to anything or anybody. For example, her boss gave her a machine for making juices, for he was fastidious and vegetarian. Ma thought the carrots weren't going round fast enough in the machine, so to help them on she stuck her finger in, the top of which got juiced with the carrots. Covering the mutilated member with a napkin, she managed to serve the juice and make it back to the office kitchen before she fainted. In hospital she came to for a few minutes.

'Thank God,' she muttered, 'it was carrots not spinach, the colour . . . so lucky . . .' She then passed out again. All this happened in the Thirties when jobs were hard to find. I don't think her boss ever knew what a potent brew he drank.

Reproduced from *Bolts from the Blue*, Hodder & Stoughton Ltd

JIM BOWEN
Comedian/Entertainer/Presenter

Funny things are always happening to me, but the most memorable are connected with 'Bullseye'. There was one show in particular when the producer, a noted practical joker, hired a stripper-gram girl to pose as a contestant! There I was during rehearsal asking her the usual questions, when suddenly she starts to take her clothes off! The audience was as stunned as me, but what gave it away was the laughter from the control room and the camera crew. They were all falling about as I flustered on and the girl ended up in bra and pants!

But that wasn't the end of it. When we got to the actual show and I had to pull the questions from the revolving drum, someone had glued them inside! And then, for a finale, Rod Hull suddenly appeared with that frightening Emu of his!! I had previously told the producer that I was terrified of appearing on TV with that overgrown budgie, and suddenly there he was — and by the look in his eyes I knew he was going to do his stuff!! I ended up on the floor with Emu biting my neck and chaos reigning in the studio. It was murder at the time, but when I look back now, it is hard to suppress a giggle!

RICHARD BRIERS

Actor

As you probably know it is not often that I attempt major parts in Shakespeare. It is always tricky to try and be serious when you have a well known face on the television, trying to make people laugh. Can you be taken seriously in a dramatic, classical role?

About fifteen years ago I appeared as *Richard III* in Glasgow. I was pretty impressive in the part, I thought. I would spellbind the audience with my first speech — '*Now is the winter of our discontent*' ... The curtain rose, and I walked slowly downstage, and with great authority spoke the first line of this great play. I got to the end of the first line, and paused for a short breath, when an old age pensioner waved at me from the fourth row of the stalls.

'Hello Richard' she yelled.

For a second I was horrified, and then realising that for better or worse I was after all a 'household name' I reluctantly waved back. I don't think she stayed till the end. There weren't enough laughs!

JANET BROWN
Comedienne

Some time ago I was shopping in a large department store and had been trying on some outfits. As I walked across to the lifts to go to another department, I saw a woman coming purposefully towards me. I immediately thought 'Ah, an autograph-hunter' and was ready with smile and pen to sign her book or piece of paper when she said: 'Excuse me but I had to tell you, you have your cardigan on inside out.'

She was absolutely right. I had been walking about the store with the label boldly on display in complete ignorance. I thanked her and quickly put the matter right, thinking that next time I would not jump to conclusions!

MICHAEL BUERK
Newscaster

The funniest thing that ever happened to me in broadcasting didn't seem too amusing at the time.

I was new to the business and was involved in a news programme where a number of contributors were sitting round a table. A short way into quite a lengthy piece, my nose started to bleed. I spluttered on manfully − spraying blood liberally all over the table and the other people, who struggled to salvage their scripts from the deluge. Just as well I was on radio at the time!

Sir Alastair Burnet

Newscaster

On 'News At Ten' one night I had to read a report on a move to try to restore corporal punishment in schools in Somerset or somewhere. By mistake I talked of restoring 'capital' punishment. I didn't notice it, so I was surprised to get many phone calls afterwards inquiring if I had had enough to drink before the programme. But I was slightly mollified to get a letter from an apparently long-suffering father, who said he'd been delighted by the news — and could I let him have a list of good schools in Somerset?

Dora Bryan

Actress

I recently heard two ladies discussing my performance. 'Isn't Dora wonderful, and she's over 80 you know.' Made me laugh!

HARRY CARPENTER

Sports Commentator

Back in the 1960s, when Billy Walker was one of our young heavyweight boxing stars, BBC-TV did a live transmission of his fight at Belle Vue, Manchester, with the Italian, Giulio Rinaldi. Billy knocked him out well inside a round. This threw our plans out quite a bit and while we got ready to proceed with the follow-up fight, the producer, Roy Lakeland said to me through my headphones:

'Jump up in the ring, Harry, and have a word with Billy. We'll turn the recording round and show it to you and Billy and he can tell you how he KO'd the Italian.'

I got up in the ring and started interviewing Billy. But when I looked down at the monitor outside the ring, a man kept waving his arms and mouthing the words: 'Not ready yet.'

So I went on talking with Billy. The replay was still not ready. I brought in Billy's brother, George, his manager, and started talking to him. No replay. I returned to Billy for more chat. Still not ready. I was running out of things to talk to Billy about. And then, a little man called Joe Rashman, who was a steward of the British Boxing Board of Control, jumped up into the ring (remember, we were 'live' on the air) and he came between me and Billy and shouted at me: 'Get out of the ring! You're holding up the show!'

I was very embarrassed. I crept through the ropes, returned to my seat, put my headphones back on, and heard Ray say: 'Sorry about that, Harry. Had a spot of trouble turning the recording round. But it's ready now. Tell the viewers what they're going to see.' So I apologised for the interrupted interview, explained that we had had some trouble and said: 'Right. Now we can see again how Billy Walker knocked out Giulio Rinaldi inside a round. Here it is.'

And up came, not the Billy Walker KO, but a recording of a flyweight fight we had recorded earlier ... and so it went on, from one disaster to another.

My worst – and funniest – experience on TV.

JOHN CARTER

Travel Journalist

During the many years I have been a travel writer, I have had many amusing experiences and encounters, but the one that comes first to mind concerns a time when I took my wife and small daughters on a villa holiday to Majorca. It was, I have to admit, very many years ago, but the memory is still strong!

We arrived at Palma airport very late one afternoon to learn that there was nobody to meet us. A message from the holiday company's rep simply instructed us to get on a bus to Palma Nova and go to a particular bar/café near the bus stop at our destination. There we would be given the key to the villa and instructions as to how to get there. We did as we were told, with some difficulty, as we had two large suitcases, two small daughters and our hand luggage. At the bar I was given the key and instructions and we set off to walk about 100 yards up a gloomy lane. By now it was getting very dark. We found the villa, but the key did not fit the front door. It didn't fit the back door, either! I didn't fancy going all the way back to get the right key, so I ended up breaking a window, letting myself into the kitchen, and then letting my wife and daughters in through the front door. By this time we were very angry, and my anger was made worse when we discovered that there was no 'welcome' assortment of provisions in the fridge (as the brochure had promised). I had to search around to find the main electricity switch, so we could have some light, but there was nothing to eat or drink. Eventually we got the children to sleep, then went to sleep ourselves.

Next morning I returned to the bar to give the barman, and the holiday rep a piece of my mind. She was there, and took the wind out of my sails by telling me her absence the previous day was because she had to take her own daughter into hospital with suspected appendicitis. When I complained about the state of the villa, she told me that she herself had put the 'welcome' provisions into the kitchen the previous morning.

Together we went to sort it out.

It was then I discovered I had broken into the wrong villa! The one we should have gone to was another few yards along the other side of the lane. The key fitted, the provisions were there, along with a note from the rep explaining her absence. The villa we had used was privately owned by a German family, who were due to arrive the next weekend. So I paid to have the window mended and, when the Germans arrived, we kept out of their way!!

KEITH CHEGWIN

Presenter

Quite a few funny things have happened to me over the years on television but I suppose the most memorable one for me was one Saturday morning during the days of 'Swap Shop.'

I was in the Roman Baths in the city of Bath and was allowed to swim in the famous spa waters. So there I was on live TV in only a pair of swimming trunks on a very cold Saturday morning. However, when I dived into the water my trunks slipped off and seven million people saw the other side of Cheggers!!

PAUL COIA

Presenter

I had the pleasure of presenting a series called 'Pebble Mill At One.' On the last programme, the street outside our studio was mobbed with viewers complaining at the axeing of the show and I was sent out to do some interviews with them.

I spotted a blue-haired punk rocker with a T-shirt emblazoned with the slogan 'Save Pebble Mill', but lost him in the crowd. I later saw him shuffling to the front, and as he turned his back I saw another slogan saying 'The Mill is Fab.'

Again I lost him in the crowd, but with 30 seconds to go, up he popped again. I shoved a microphone in front of him to get his thoughts on the show. I asked the camera to zoom in on his shirt, and asked him to turn round to see the message written on his back. He refused several times. With five million people watching on LIVE TV, I couldn't let him get away with it, so I asked his friends to spin him round. The camera caught the slogan in glorious close-up – but one problem. I'd got hold of the wrong punk!

The slogan, seen by five million viewers read 'SHOW US YOUR TITS MARIAN'!

PATTIE COLDWELL

Presenter

When I was a junior reporter at Granada Television I was invited to dinner by an old friend with nine men! I was holding court and having a great time when a very famous film director came to join us. He was one of those people who whenever I met him made me terribly nervous and I always did something stupid when he was watching.

On this occasion I decided not to let him rattle me! I carried on nattering twenty to the dozen to the assembled crowd and tried to ignore him. Someone suggested I was holding up the meal 'cos I was still eating my spare ribs and everyone had finished. He was staring at me and waiting, it seemed, for me to make a fool of myself — and I didn't let him down! Instead of finishing my spare rib quickly, I leaned over to dip it in what I thought was hot sauce — and quickly realised I'd dipped it in the fingerbowl that everyone had just washed their hands in. As I nonchalantly ate every mouthful I realised he'd seen it all and was smirking contentedly across the table. My evening was ruined and I can never eat spare ribs now without blushing! That'll teach me to stop trying to impress important people — it never works!

JOHN COLE
Political Editor

In 1984, I had a coronary by-pass operation in April, returned to work in July, but was really supposed to be treating myself gently when the party conferences came round in the Autumn. Then, on the last night of the Conservative Conference at Brighton, the bomb went off at the Grand Hotel, with tragic consequences. I tumbled out of bed at an adjoining hotel at 3 a.m. interviewed the Prime Minister outside the police station at about 4 a.m. worked right through the day until the 9 o'clock television news that night, and reached home at midnight.

The following week was my check-up at the Westminster Hospital. The Sister eyed me suspiciously: 'I saw you interviewing Mrs Thatcher in the dark last week!'

I explained the circumstances.

'Then I saw you on the news late the same evening. Was that live or recorded?'

'Live, Sister,' I said to this young woman, fully as old as my second child.

'Well,' she said sternly, 'that's not the way we told you to behave, is it?'

I later told this story to the consultant, who laughed.

'Doubtless all our patients are behaving less sensibly than we advise,' he said. 'But if you insist on doing it in front of cameras, you must expect to be told off.'

SUE COOK
Presenter

I had been working as a radio presenter for some years, making only the occasional appearances on TV, when I was asked to audition for my first TV series. In a state of excitement and nerves, I sat on the train from London to Manchester where the headquarters of BBC Childrens' Programmes is.

About twenty other people were also auditioning for the job, and I waited my turn, sure in the knowledge that they were far better than I was, and fighting the strong urge to rush out of the building back to the station and home.

At last I was on. I introduced some films, reading from the 'autocue,' gave my prepared talk on a good day out for the family at a butterfly farm and interviewed two small boys about their hobby of kite flying. So far, not *so* bad. Now, the grand finale, the *piece de resistance*. I was to show the viewers how to make their very own kite. I walked nervously to a table on which were set out a diamond-shaped piece of coloured plastic, three sticks of wood, a long piece of household string and a hole punch. Along with the other candidates I'd watched a demonstration earlier that morning. The question was — could I remember it? The cameras closed in. I hoped the bright smile I attempted in their direction assured everyone that this was going to be a piece of cake. No problem. Privately I didn't believe a word of it.

'Right.' I picked up the piece of plastic and the hole punch. 'First, punch a hole in each of the two opposite corners.' I inserted the plastic into the machine, punched, and looked at the result. A half-moon shape. I smiled rather too widely at the camera. Tried again. Another half-moon. I tried again — another half-moon. Better move on, I thought, trying my this-is-easy smile at the camera again, and punching three more half-moon shapes in the other side too. Better tackle the bits of wood, I thought desperately. 'Now,' I said, in a voice I suddenly recognised as pure Joyce Grenfell, 'glue this long stick along here, and these two shorter ones here, like

so, then ... take your piece of string ...' I designed the
tone of my voice to show that it was almost done, 'and ...
ah ...' The string seemed to take on a life of its own as
I picked it up. It became an instant mass of knots. I had
another go at that bright smile. I seem to remember words
coming out of my mouth, but goodness knows what I said.
I was desperately picking at the knots with my fingers and
teeth. At last, knots undone, I announced with ill-
concealed pure relief 'Finally, simply thread your string
through the holes you have made in your ...' (smile of
triumph fades on face) 'the holes you've made in your er
...' I seized the punch for one final futile attempt at the
perfect hole 'the holes ... you *should* have made in ... er
... well ... that's-sort-of-how-you-make-a-kite-from-me-
goodbye-for-now.' (and definitely for ever) I thought as I
wandered weakly off the set.

For some reason that will always escape me, they gave me
the job. My career in television began. I'll never forget that
first and only TV audition though!

PAT COOMBS

Actress

Way back in 1969 I was experiencing my first real success
— a series (BBC-TV) called 'Beggar My Neighbour',
starring June Whitfield, Peter Jones, Reg Varney — and me!
We lived, then, in Haywards Heath, Sussex and I was a
frequent visitor to the local library. One Monday morning,
a dreary, dull, grey, wet day, I ventured forth to said library
with my beloved Mum's words ringing in my ears . . . 'O!
You *do* look poor . . .!'

I was suitably dressed in drab, 'wet day clothes' . . . sort
of beigey-brown all over! As I toured the bookshelves I was
aware of a small girl following me everywhere — and finally
at the 'out' counter she was there again with her mum
beside her. She leaned towards me and then whispered to
mother, 'That lady was on television last night' (True!) . . .
Mother looked me up and down and sideways — taking in
the beige look — turned to daughter and said loudly, 'No!
I shouldn't think so dear . . .!' I felt so sorry for that
youngster! But I was rooted to the spot and I couldn't bring
my beige — dull — self to say, 'You're right!!'

JILLY COOPER
Author

My daughter Emily got a rather awful report one year from her boarding school when she was eleven.

You can imagine our amazement, therefore when a week or so later we got a letter from the school saying:

'Dear Mr and Mrs Cooper, Congratulations, your daughter has just been awarded a scholarship of £1,000 a year.'

I was in ecstasies, the darling girl hadn't failed us after all.

Then I read down the page, to discover they were referring to 'your daughter Heidi'. They'd got the *wrong* Coopers. So Leo, my husband, who's a publisher by profession, wrote a marvellously wicked letter back, saying actually our daughter was called Emily. He wasn't aware he had a daughter called Heidi, could she possibly be the result of an indiscretion at the Frankfurt bookfair eleven years ago? By return of post we got a letter back, saying very tartly: HEIDI WAS BORN IN BELGIUM.

JIMMY CRICKET
Comedian

I remember I was in hospital once in Belfast. I said to the Sister in charge of the ward:

'Sister,' says I, 'I noticed that on some of the beds there's a letter "P" and on some others there's the letters "R.C." That doesn't mean that some beds are for Protestants and some for Roman Catholics?'

She said, 'No, Jimmy. Some patients are having porridge for breakfast and some patients are having rice crispies.'

LESLIE CROWTHER

Actor/Comedian

Like most little boys, I developed the usual healthy interest in the opposite sex. I spent hours wondering what they looked like without their clothes on. The fact that one could see little girls wandering about in local paddling pools, or by the seaside, stark naked, was unimpressive. They were only toddlers, so they didn't count! It was one's contemporaries at school that one mentally stripped in the playground. I had my first break at the age of eight, when a nubile young lady of the same age — or maybe a year or two older — virtually picked me up in the school holidays, and invited herself round for tea.

My mother suggested that we should go upstairs and play in my bedroom after tea; a suggestion that Deirdre Bosworth seized upon eagerly. You see, I even remember her name! Once upstairs, she offered me a tour of inspection. Breathlessly I accepted her offer, and she divested herself of her blouse and vest.

'Those are called breasts,' she declared.

I was not impressed. I'd seen fat boys in the showers who were bigger than she was! This is probably why, when I was twelve and at a co-educational school in Twickenham, I evolved MY PLAN. Not only were the girls of my age infinitely shapelier by then, but we all used to go to the same public swimming baths for swimming lessons. Our changing rooms were divided by a wooden screen which started at the ceiling but didn't quite reach the ground. The kind of gap that enterprising West Indians are said to limbo underneath and so get in free! I bought a pocket mirror and instructed my mates to do the same. At the next opportunity, we placed the mirrors in a row on the floor under the screen which divided us from the girls, and by skilfully tilting them we saw the lot! The following week we were surprised to hear sounds of uncontrolled mirth coming from the other side of the screen. Staring aghast at the floor, we saw a row of mirrors tilted towards us. It wasn't their retaliation that rankled — it was their laughter! Mind you, it was a very cold day!

MARK CURRY

Presenter/Actor

Quite some time ago I was travelling from Leeds to Wakefield on the train. As I was getting off at Wakefield a man in front of me was struggling with quite a few cases, so I asked him should I take the large one in front of me. He replied,

'Yes, if you like.' So I did. IT WAS HEAVY!!!

He motioned for me to carry it down the platform and through the ticket barrier, which I did. We reached the exit of the station which leads you out onto the car park and I was still struggling with the case and he motioned me out towards the car park. When we got there he said to me,

'Which is your car?'

I replied, 'I haven't got one.'

He said, 'What are you going to do with that case?'

I said, 'Leave it here for you.'

He replied, 'But it's not MY case.'

I gasped, 'Well why did you keep telling me to follow you?'

He said, 'I thought you didn't know where you were going!'

It had all been a terrible misunderstanding, me thinking that this poor guy needed help with HIS case when some poor person was probably travelling all the way to London safe in the knowledge that his or her stuff was travelling too!! How wrong they were. I left the case, which felt like it was filled with tins of baked beans, safe in the hands of a ticket man. I've been a bit more reluctant to help people off trains since!!

BERNARD DAVEY

Weatherman

I suppose all the funny things that have happened to me surround my short time on television as a weatherman. After a two-week holiday in Ireland I said it was nice to be back, the weather wasn't up to much, but the crack was good. ('Crack' here means talk, banter, jokes with family and friends). After the broadcast several people who didn't understand that meaning rang up to ask if the weatherman was on drugs. ('Crack'= type of drug!)

DIANA DAVIES

Mrs Bates in Emmerdale Farm

My story happened when my son Stephen, now 25, was about 14 years old and was very late for school one morning. I leapt into the car in nightie, housecoat and slippers, backed out of the drive, over his home-made go-cart, drove to his school, thinking the car wasn't steering too well, and finally let him out. As he ran towards the school he shouted nonchalantly over his shoulder, 'Mum, you've got a flat tyre.'

There I was absolutely stranded in my none-too-attractive nightwear. Luckily for me a father of one of the pupils spotted the flat tyre and came to my window to tell me about it. He then of course noticed that I wasn't in my tyre-changing outfit and, like a gent, jacked the car up and changed the tyre with me inside, otherwise I think I'd have been there still and then who would have looked after Mr Turner?

P.S. I can't change tyres anyway.

DAME JUDI DENCH

O.B.E.

Actress

When I was doing *Anthony and Cleopatra* at the National Theatre last year, we used a live snake. As we played in repertoire, it sometimes happened that there would be quite a long break between performances. During a performance just after one such break, I reached the point where I had to put the snake to my breast and, being somewhat out of practice, didn't do it exactly as I had before; but everything seemed fine. At the end of the play as I was waiting to do my curtain call, I could feel something very odd going on in my wig. I put my hand up and felt ... the snake! It was impossible to get rid of it before the call, and there I was, bowing and smiling, trying not to let on that I was wearing a snake in my hair! I don't know if this is a funny story — especially if you don't like snakes — but I have laughed about it since that occasion.

DAVID DIMBLEBY

Interviewer/Presenter

The first interview I ever did with the present Prime Minister, Mrs Margaret Thatcher, was in Washington just after her appointment as Leader of the Conservative Party. She was very keen, for obvious reasons, to be filmed with the White House in the background.

Unfortunately there was only one place where this could be done: in Lafayette Park. There is also only one bench on which the interviewee, but not the interviewer can sit. Mrs Thatcher was in a rush and I looked for a suitable support to film the interview. I took the plastic container from one of the dustbins in the park and, turning it upside down, sat on top. The interview began. As I reached the end of my first question the container collapsed and I fell to the ground. We cut the camera but the delays were embarrassing. Mrs Thatcher was in a hurry for her next appointment. There was no alternative but to conduct the interview in order that we should seem to be looking straight at each other, with me on my knees. This would have been alright because no viewer would have known. Unfortunately a passing British tourist took a photograph and later sent it not to me, but to Mrs Thatcher. Downing Street now has a photograph which shows the two of us, Mrs Thatcher sitting grandly on her bench and me meekly kneeling in front of her. I have no doubt some of her staunchest supporters think this is the proper attitude for a political interviewer to take up, but I rather wish the photograph had been sent to me, not her.

FRED DINENAGE

Presenter

On an ITV sports programme, a few years ago, I was introducing the football manager, Lawrie McMenemy — our studio guest — with the words: 'And our guest tonight is football's man-of-the-moment, the magical Lawrie McMenemy ...'

As it turned out, there were just too many 'm's in one sentence, and I stumbled badly over the word McMenemy. I just couldn't seem to say it ... and the harder I tried, the worse it got.

In the end, in my annoyance with myself, I said — unfortunately loud enough for everyone to hear — 'Oh! What a pillock!' (Pillock being an old-fashioned word for fool).

Unfortunately, at that precise moment when I said 'pillock,' the camera focussed on the face of Lawrie himself. The viewers — and Lawrie — all thought I'd called HIM a pillock. And, as he's well over six feet tall, that would have been quite a stupid thing to do!

It took quite a long time — and a few 'repeat fees' from showings on 'It'll Be Alright On The Night' — before Lawrie really forgave me. Even now, when he rings me up, he always says:

'Hallo Fred, it's Pillock here!'

CLIVE DUNN

Actor

In the gents' loo in the Leicester Square Theatre a man asked me:
'Are you Clive Dunn at all?'

PAUL EDDINGTON

Actor

Having an easily recognisable face can have its drawbacks.
I went into a shop once and the assistants crowded round for an autograph.
When I came to pay for my purchase the manager said:
'Can I see some form of identification, please?'

JANET ELLIS

Presenter/Actress

Recently, I attended a school fête 'incognito.' As I walked round the stalls I saw a little boy tugging his mother's sleeve. He whispered something in her ear.

'He says you look just like Janet from "Blue Peter"', she told me amazed. 'Now that's a compliment, isn't it?!'

MICHAEL FISH

Weatherman

The only incidents I recall are when a main fuse in the studio blew and it was plunged into darkness, and when a cleaner (complete with working Hoover) burst in during a radio broadcast.

BRYAN FORBES

Actor/Writer/Director

In 1948 I had the great good fortune to appear with Gertrude Lawrence in a play by Daphne du Maurier called *September Tide* which ran at the Aldwych Theatre. The play also starred Michael Gough and Anne Leon and ran to packed houses for nine months. It was the last appearance of Miss Lawrence on an English stage.

I had an arrangement with Michael Gough whereby I partly shared the services of his dresser, an engaging and eccentric character named Herbert. Herbert's principle responsibility came in the second act when Micky had to dive from the balcony of the house into the harbour to rescue the drifting boat. He dived, of course, into a pile of mattresses strategically placed off-stage and out of sight of the audience. He then had to plunge into a bath of lukewarm water to simulate the real thing for his reappearance. Herbert had to be standing by to assist.

During one matinee when the Aldwych was packed with middle-aged matrons all balancing tea trays on their knees, one of the cleats securing Michael Relph's weighty set suddenly gave way. Ossie, the stage manager, dashed in search of stage-hands to repair the damage before the set caved in. Now it so happened that this incident took place a few minutes before Micky was due to make his celebrated plunge into the harbour. Herbert was waiting in the wings and before he disappeared Ossie handed him a support rope and told him to hang on to it until help arrived.

Meanwhile on-stage Gertie and Micky continued with the scene, unaware of the drama being enacted in the wings. Micky leapt from the balcony and groped his way in the semi-darkness to the bath of water.

During his absence Gertie went to a cupboard in the supposedly totally deserted house and took some towels out in readiness for Micky's drenched return. It was a vital plot point and carefully established in the dialogue that she and her son-in-law were isolated and alone – the storm

Unbeknown to Gertie, Herbert was standing holding the rope on the other side of the cupboard door. It was a hot afternoon and he was curiously dressed in pin-stripe trousers, collarless shirt and white tennis shoes. I should also add that he had a small Hitler moustache. The total effect was startling.

Gertie opened the cupboard door as she had done for the last two hundred performances and revealed Herbert. She was too dumbfounded to close the door again, and for a few seconds she and Herbert stood transfixed like characters in a Disney cartoon. Herbert, being of the old school of theatrical dressers, was also a stickler for etiquette. He couldn't help himself. He gave a little bow and said, 'Good afternoon, Miss Lawrence.' Up to this point the audience had been mystified but not unduly alarmed by this sudden plot twist. After all, since they hadn't seen the play before, it was conceivable that Miss du Maurier had intended that her central character be suddenly confronted with Hitler in tennis shoes inside a cupboard.

But when Herbert had paid his respects to Miss Lawrence the game was up. Gertie managed to close the door and then started to collapse. She turned away up-stage in a futile attempt to conceal her mounting hysteria and, of course, minus towels, bumped straight into a wet and unsuspecting Micky. He clambered back over the balcony and was greeted with a howl of laughter from the audience and a leading lady staggering around as though inexplicably drunk. In such circumstances an actor's first instinct is to check his flies, which Micky did. Finding that everything was intact, he began his dialogue as per cue, but received no answering cue for by now Gertie — one of the world's great gigglers — was on the floor. Micky assumed that she had gone temporarily insane and carried on, giving her dialogue as well as his own and attempting to retrieve the situation. Needing a towel, he went back to the cupboard. Renewed hysteria, this time in anticipation, from the audience. Micky opened the cupboard door. The cupboard was bare. And so the second act staggered to its conclusion, Micky having to wait until curtain-fall for an explanation.

I know many a star who would have reacted in anger to

such a situation and had the polite and unfortunate Herbert fired on the spot, but Gertie loved a joke.

Years later I was reminded of the events of that afternoon, for the second act of *September Tide* seemed accident prone. I went to see a performance of the play by a touring company. Gertie's and Michael's original roles were being played by a couple who were perhaps a little long in the tooth. The gentleman wore a toupee in an effort to help credibility. The moment came in the second act when the famous omelet had to be cooked. The woman left the stage for a few moments to fetch a bottle of Nuits St George while the husband stirred the concoction in the omelet pan. To everybody's stunned horror, as he bent over his task the toupee came unstuck and dropped into the mess of eggs. He stirred it in. The wife returned, gay and expectant, prepared to play a tender scene with a young lover, and found herself confronted with a demented bald headed old man cooking a pan of hairy eggs which eventually they would have to eat. It was almost too painful to watch.

An extract from *Notes for a Life* published by Collins in 1974, copyright Bryan Forbes Limited.

SARAH GREENE

Presenter/Actress

I'd only just got started on 'Blue Peter' and was wearing a brand new pair of white shoes. As I was doing an extremely long and concentrated item to camera, I felt a very strange sensation on my left foot. The tortoise had taken a fancy to my shoe, presumably believing it to be a female tortoise and was showing his affection in no uncertain terms!! All I could do was keep talking and keep smiling.

SIMON GROOM

Presenter

Back in 1978, when I had just joined 'Blue Peter,' with Goldie who was then only a few weeks old, I was leaving the studio after only my fourth appearance, when a somewhat embarrassing experience occurred. Unknown to me, H.M. The Queen was visiting the studios at Television Centre to watch a performance of 'The Good Life' and was due to arrive any moment. As I made my way from the 'Blue Peter' studio with Goldie and my bags into the main reception, I was greeted by a barrage of lights and cameras, and dozens of high-ranking BBC officials in dinner dress waiting nervously for the Queen's arrival.

As I left my dressing room key at the desk, I glanced down to see Goldie (who was not toilet-trained yet) squatting in the middle of the reception area and depositing a huge puddle which was spreading across the floor!!

We were quickly bundled out by the BBC executives and as I went through the door, I glanced round to see them mopping up the offending 'water' with their dress handkerchiefs, seconds before the Royal car pulled up. Goldie and I escaped just in time!

MICHAEL GROTH
Presenter/Musician

It was in 1978 I think. I had a six-piece band called Valentino, and we were on tour in Germany for two weeks. While we were at a very nice town called Mannheim, I met a lovely girl and got on with her extremely well. The evening came to an end, I wrote her address on an empty cigarette packet and thought I would get in touch with her when I got home. About a month later, back in London, I found a cigarette packet with this German name and address on it, it was something like *Gerhild Bauer*, a very odd name.

So I wrote a lovely letter, saying how much I'd enjoyed the evening, and asking her over to stay with me. I told her I had only one bed, but I didn't mind if she didn't mind, etc., etc.

A week went by and I received a reply. It said:

> 'Dear Michael,
> Thank you for your kind invitation, which, I must say, surprised me somewhat. Unfortunately, I don't think I can make it in the foreseeable future, as I'm rather busy managing the disco.'

I had written to the MALE manager of a disco in which we'd played. I'd obviously got the wrong cigarette pack!!

TERRY HALL(and LENNY THE LION)

Ventriloquist

My funniest moment came when I was appearing in pantomime a few years ago and happened to mention that Lenny was fed every day at 2 p.m. and loved sausages. I didn't think any more about it until the next day when, bang on 2 p.m., a little lad of no more than six or seven turned up at the stage door of the theatre with a bag containing one pound of best pork sausages, which had obviously come from his mother's fridge! I could hardly keep the smile from my face as I explained to the little lad that Lenny was having a nap and his sausages were specially flown in from the jungle! I suggested that he go home and put the sausages back before his mum missed them, and made a mental note never to mention such things again on stage. I often wonder how he got on when he returned home, but I've had many a giggle about it ever since!

DAVID HAMILTON
Broadcaster

One day my girlfriend and I went shopping, an exercise which I always find particularly boring. While she was browsing endlessly around the store unable to make a decision about what to purchase, I decided to stand in the window along with the dummies to amuse myself with the comments of the passers-by.

After remarks like 'I didn't know they sold men's clothes here' and 'I don't think much of that blazer,' an old lady said 'Oh look, that dummy looks just like David Hamilton.'

JUDITH HANN
Writer/Presenter

Some of the funniest situations are when people 'think' they recognise me.

Once — on a family holiday in California — my two young sons were just saying how nice it was to be in a non-'Tomorrow's World'-watching country (Europe, Hong Kong, New Zealand etc all see 'Tomorrow's World'), because we were not being stopped for autographs.

At that very moment a group of merry (post-lunch) English tourists staggered towards me shouting,

'We know who you are!'

Then, prodding me on the shoulder, 'You can't deny it, you're Miriam Stoppard.'

You can guess my nickname for the rest of the holiday.

ROLF HARRIS
O.B.E.

Entertainer/Singer/Songwriter/Musician
Artist/Cartoonist

One of the funniest things I can remember was when I was doing a guest appearance on a big chat show in Canada and I was to sing 'Tie Me Kangaroo Down, Sport' – out I came with my wobble board, which as you may know is a chunk of hardboard about two feet by three feet, and sanded down so it's a bit thinner than normal.

Well, there I was, just introduced, and I propped the board on the stage to have the obligatory chat and suddenly as I went to put a little weight on the board it just vertically disappeared – I almost overbalanced, looked down, and there is a slot about an eighth of an inch wide where two sections of the stage are joined, and its gone straight down to the basement – one minute it's there – next it's not.

Imagine trying to explain that to an audience who didn't actually see what happened. The long wait for someone to go down and get it. It seemed interminable. It was good to laugh at it afterwards, but at the time ... oh boy!

TONY HART

Artist

In the 60s I worked on a television series that entailed bringing a live animal into the studio every week and drawing it. Each time something pretty devastating occurred so on the occasion that I brought a male skunk to the set the effect was more than chaotic. At rehearsal the skunk, although said to have been doctored, took exception to being my model and made his feelings felt in the way he knew best. It was pretty potent. My reaction was to cough and splutter thereby holding everything up. The producer, safe in the gallery pressed his talk-back button and somewhat tetchily said 'Tony, stop mucking about and get on with it.' Aggrieved, I muttered that it was impossible to work in the present situation. 'Rubbish' came the reply. 'I'm coming down.' Clattering down the steps and striding across the studio floor he said 'Now what's all this nonsense, there's absolutely nothing . . . Aggggh!' Clamping his hand over his nose and mouth he retreated to the gallery inarticulately demanding cans of aerosol spray stuff. The ghastly miasma hung around for all too long while rehearsal continued. A group called the Swinging Blue Jeans took up their position in exactly the same spot where I had been. With their colourful costume, long hair and instruments they crashed into their act seemingly impervious to the situation.

There's a sequel to all this. Only a week later I was doing another television programme at the old Riverside Studios. Queuing up for tea at the crush bar I saw the well known colourful costumes, long hair and instruments. 'Hello, nice to see you again,' I said. 'Sorry about the skunk in Manchester.' 'You what?' asked the one with the longest hair. 'The skunk. In the studio. The awful smell,' I reminded him. 'What smell, dad?' I left it at that but was telling the whole story to a friend who was on the same programme that day. 'Quite a coincidence seeing the Swinging Blue Jeans again here.' 'Tony' he said pityingly 'They're the Rolling Stones.'

NIGEL HAWTHORNE
Actor

I was working just outside Vienna on *Firefox*, which starred
Clint Eastwood who was also directing the film. We were
doing night shoots at a military aerodrome some way away
and, on this particular evening, I had expected to be
working all night. To my astonishment Clint Eastwood and
the producer, Fritz Manes, came up to me and said 'Go back
to the hotel and sleep. See you tomorrow.'

As it was only just after midnight I was taken completely
off balance. 'Really?' I squawked, 'how marvellous. Well —
thank you and goodnight Cliff and Felix.'

They looked at me oddly and I blushed with the
realisation, compounding it by adding 'That's silly, I know
that those aren't your names. You're ... em ...'

They smiled at one another in a bemused sort of way and
tactfully moved off to check the lighting for the next scene,
leaving me wondering whether, under different circumstances, I might have called Winston Churchill 'Wilfred' or
Bernard Shaw 'Barry.' Mind you, I'd have been alright with
the Two Ronnies.

PHILIP HAYTON

Newscaster

Life on the news can be very bleak. But I did hear an amusing tale from a friend in Beirut. He was aboard a Middle East Airlines plane when it landed safely amid shelling of the airport. As the plane taxied to the terminal the passengers applauded the pilot. He said over the public address system: 'Thank you very much for flying with us today. We look forward to your next trip. Good Evening.'

Then, forgetting to turn off his microphone, he added: 'Now all I need is a large whisky and a good woman.'

The stewardess tidying up in the galley became alarmed about what he might say next. She started to rush towards the cockpit when an elderly woman passenger grabbed her by the arm, saying: 'Don't rush, give him time to finish his whisky!'

PAUL HEINEY

Presenter

A few years ago, at the time when I was a reporter on Radio One's 'Newsbeat', I was asked by the editor to go down to a West End hotel where the contestants in that year's 'Miss World' contest were gathering.

The story centred around Miss Rhodesia who was involved in a political row and there was a suggestion that she might be banned from the contest. I was sent to get the first radio interview with her. Needless to say, the press had gathered and the hotel suite was crawling with reporters and photographers. I explained that my deadline was only an hour away and so one of the organisers got hold of me in one hand, and the stunning Miss Rhodesia in the other and said, 'You'll need somewhere quiet. Get in there.' At which point he opened a door, shoved us both in and slammed it shut. It was the lavatory! We both tried very hard to ignore it, did our interview, and when I opened the door, at least a dozen Fleet Street press men were gathered round it, some bent to the lock trying to overhear.

Next day, I scanned the papers for 'BBC Man in Beauty Lav Lock Up' but thankfully there were none.

However, the memory of Miss Rhodesia still lives on.

JIMMY HILL

Presenter

'A GRAY IS A GRAY'

A long time ago now, Ted Edgar, the well known international showjumper, taught me to ride a horse. In the early weeks, as those of you who have been through the same process will understand only too well, the knack didn't come all that easily. But there came a time when I was almost competent enough to be allowed to ride alone without supervision. On Ted's advice I had bought a gray mare, Girlie being her day-to-day name and Snow White her posh name, largely for the benefit of my then three-year-old daughter. Girlie was a splendid animal and safely carried me over many an obstacle in the Warwickshire countryside, but more than that, she was quiet to ride at all times and sometimes as a treat, I would sit daughter, Joanna, on her back with me and gently walk around Ted's paddock.

One weekend when Ted and his wife, Liz, were due to travel away for a showjumping competition somewhere in England, Ted mentioned that if I wanted to come up and ride Girlie in his absence, she would be in the field by the Church just opposite his Warwickshire farmhouse. 'You know how to tack her up by now,' he said, 'just help yourself and come over and enjoy a ride if you feel like it.'

So on Sunday morning I set off with Joanna to the farm and took a pail with a few nuts in it to catch Girlie. I was surprised how quickly she came, because if she had a vice it was that she was not easy to catch, especially by an untrained innocent! Having patted myself on the back for having caught her so quickly, I led her across the yard, tacked her up and thought that to start the proceedings, before giving Joanna her Sunday morning ride, I'd have a hop or two over a couple of jumps left up in the paddock. I thought when I started to canter the mare after warming her up for a bit that she seemed to be rather more springy than usual and her whole action was more rhythmic. I imagined that either Ted or Liz had been schooling her and had produced a much smoother ride as a result. However, when I came to jump a couple of poles for the first time, she stopped suddenly and started to rear, which rather surprised me, because she had never behaved badly in similar circumstances before. So I gave her a little talking to and turned round ready to jump again. By this time she was beginning to get very hot and to rear and jump and buck and do all sorts of things not easy to cope with as a result of my limited experience. This went on for several minutes and in the end I gave in. 'Maybe I won't jump this morning,' I reasoned. 'I'll just give Joanna her little walk round.' So, Joanna was sitting on a gate at the edge of the field and I started to walk Girlie gently over to the gate so that I could lift Joanna onto her back. But I couldn't get Girlie to go anywhere near the gate, or to do anything else right for that matter. After several minutes of trying I decided that she was in no mood to co-operate on that morning and the best thing I could do was to put her back in the stable and make sure that both father and daughter went home to Sunday lunch uninjured. That's exactly what I did.

It was a day or two later when I mentioned the incident to Ted and asked him if he could explain why my mild and good-mannered hunter had behaved so irrationally on that Sunday morning. I wasn't prepared for the burst of laughter that followed, which went on for some time. Ted had realised that the mare I had thought was Girlie in the field by the Church was in fact a highly neurotic and frisky, similar-looking mare called Blue, whom even he had difficulty in controlling, and who just could not be trusted. It wasn't until that moment that I had any idea that I had not been riding my own mare. When it came to horses and riding, I always believed everything Professor Ted told me implicitly. As far as I was concerned, if Ted said that Girlie was going to be in a field on a Sunday morning, then that was that – I never let another possibility enter my head. Mind you, if Blue had been a chestnut ...!?

VINCE HILL

Entertainer

Suzi Quatro and I were asked to do a lunchtime programme for ITV called 'Gas Street', and, naturally enough, *TV Times* wanted to shoot a set of pictures for a feature article. At this point, photographer Paul Stokes enters the story. He's a great photographer and responsible for many of the super photos that you see in *TV Times*.

My wife, Annie, had the brilliant idea that Suzi and I swap styles for the photo — Suzi would wear the smart sophisticated outfit and I would wear the tight black leathers. All went well until on the day of the photo session I had to get into the tight black leathers — and believe me they were tight! I managed to squeeze into them and made my way to the massive motor bike that Paul had ordered for the shot, at the same time contemplating the prospect of spending the rest of my singing career at least one octave higher. Well, I manfully swung my leg over the saddle to the accompaniment of a deafening ripping sound and a sudden draught in my nether regions! And that's the story of why every single shot of me in that photo session is very carefully taken from the front.

THORA HIRD
O.B.E.
Actress/Comedienne

Many years ago I was involved in a serious car accident. My face hit the windscreen so you can imagine that as I lay in hospital my face was not only about a foot wide but it was bruised blue, purple, yellow, pink and black. Not a pretty sight!

A young woman was brought into the next bed for a simple appendix job . . . her aunt was with her and kept assuring her: 'There's nothing to be afraid of Elsie' . . . well, Elsie wasn't *afraid* but by the time Auntie had deposited four brown paper bags of fruit on the locker — assuring her all the time 'there's nothing to be afraid of!' Elsie *was* getting a spot nervous. Eventually, it was time for Auntie to go . . . and after informing Elsie that she 'would not be allowed to eat the pears and plums until after the "op"' she added, 'And don't forget Elsie . . . there's nothing to be nervous about!'

As she moved from the bed she caught sight of me. She did a double take and then approached me and put her lips about two inches from my ear. 'Is it Thora?' she bawled. I weakly nodded my head. 'OOO, wotta sight,' she said, 'Wotta sample!!' Then, again bending down and bawling into my ear, she said (and I must confess it restored my sense of humour) 'What a good job you were never good looking before!!'

BOB HOLNESS

Radio/Television Presenter

My silly story dates back many years, to the time when I was something of a practical joker in my youth. (That *shows* you how long ago it was!) I used to spend most of my pocket money sending away for tricks which, in those days, were widely advertised in the comics and young folks' magazines. Some came separately; some in boxes. Imagine ... a BOX full of things like imitation broken eggs, ink blots, black-eye-producing novelties which one had to hold up to the light and look through, leaving a neat circle of black around the eye ... rubber-leaded pencils; the imagination ran riot!

A small clique of us were also fans of the Marx brothers, Hellzapoppin, and later the Goons, from whom we took most of our visual gags. One of the most successful of these was the 'man-down-a-drain' illusion. It worked the very first time a couple of us tried it and the memory is still pretty clear.

We were walking down a road in Folkestone (in the holiday season) feeling fairly light-hearted (none of us drank at that stage, either!), when I came to a halt over a large storm drain. Having always been a bit of a dab hand at voices, I called down the drain, asking whether everything was all right. Then I put on a tiny voice and cried, 'No ... I can't get out!' There were one or two glances from passers-by ... more so when a regular conversation ensued. A small crowd started to collect (they had nothing else to do in Folkestone). All of a sudden I felt a nudge from one of my pals. A figure in blue was on his way over. Time to slide quietly away: which we were able to do, as most of the attention was directed down the hole in the road! Although we didn't perform this gag very many times, it was always the most successful. People's curiosity knows no bounds. The only trouble is that we were never able to see the culmination of it all. Did anyone ever prise up the drain to get the poor unfortunate feller out? We never discovered.

JIMMY HOOD

Member of Parliament for Clydesdale

(Jimmy Hood is the organiser of an
All Party Parliamentary Group on M.E.)

I can remember as a twelve-year old I won a Burns solo
singing competition with my then boy soprano voice.
When I went up to receive my prize a well known wit in
the class was heard to say to his friend, 'With a voice like
that Jimmy should be with Carouso.' His friend
immediately turned to him and said, 'Well that's nice but
where is Carouso?'

To which the classroom wit replied, 'He's dead.'

ROY HUDD

Comedian

I think the best 'ad lib' I ever heard was from my ex-
manager Michael Harvey. We were at a special televised
concert commemorating the fiftieth anniversary of the
RAF. One of the compères of the show was the late Richard
Burton (he was married to Elizabeth Taylor at the time). At
the end of the show we were all being lined up to meet
Prince Philip and Burton roared out, 'Has anyone seen my
wife?'

To which, Michael Harvey replied in a cool George
Sanders type voice: 'I'm not sure, what does she look like?'

DAVID ICKE

Sports Presenter

I asked a London hotel if they would get me a taxi to Waterloo Station. When it arrived I walked outside expecting to step into a black cab. Instead, the carriage awaiting me was a battered, rust-ridden Hillman Avenger, last seen on the Antiques Road Show. 'Oh,' I thought, taken aback, 'still, as long as it goes all will be well.'

I climbed in the back, trying to avoid the worst of the grime on the seat.

'Hello mate,' came the cheery greeting from the front. 'Where yer going then?'

'Er Waterloo Station please.'

'Waterloo ... where is that exactly?'

WHAT?

I should have got out at that point, but I stayed with it.

'Do you know the Houses of Parliament?' I said.

'I think so' he says. He thought so!

'Well if you get there, you just cross the river and there is Waterloo Station.'

'Right' he says and proceeds to spend ten minutes thumbing through his *A to Z*.

'Er 'scuse me' I said, 'the train I want leaves today, do you think we could make a move?'

'Oh right, we'll get off.'

He then called on the radio to ask where Waterloo Station was and after a period of stunned silence he was issued with a few choice words from the other end.

Anyway, before too long, we are in the middle lane going into Central London on the A40 with a stream of traffic either side of us and behind us in the rush hour. Suddenly, he stops the car, turns the engine off, and runs away down the road. I'm sitting there, slipping lower in the seat, hiding my face. Apparently he has spotted a black cab on the outside lane further down the road and he's gone off to ask him the way to Waterloo. There are people banging on the window by the time he gets back to get the car moving again.

'I've got it now,' he says. 'I've got to turn right at Baker Street.' Ages later, the train I wanted long since gone, we stop at the lights at Baker Street, one of the best known streets in London, of course. The driver turns round: 'Which one's Baker Street, mate, do you know?' At which point, I asked him if he knew the way to the nearest kerb. If so would he please park his car there so I could get out.

'Sorry, mate', he says, 'I don't know London very well!' Never.

On that same morning, when I did get a train, I sat down at a table and before I read my newspaper I thought I'd answer some letters. About an hour later, as I was finishing the letters, a massive pile of waste paper and envelopes had mounted up on the table.

The guard came along: 'Are you finished with that paper?' he says.

'Yes' I replied, thinking that all this sending employees to charm schools was working, 'thank you very much.'

'Right' he says, picks up my *Daily Mirror* and disappears through the door.

The day got better after that!

JOHN INMAN
Actor/Entertainer

Quite a few years ago I was Stage Manager on a tour of a play called *White the Sea Shines*.

As we arrived in Blackpool (my home town) to open at the Grand Theatre we learnt that the train carrying our furniture for the play had been derailed: we had a set but no furniture. As the stage manager it was my job to find some, so being home for that week the easiest way was to empty my mother's front room.

I took a van and while my mother was at work I loaded up the contents of her sitting room, took them to the Grand Theatre and set them out on the stage, after which I returned home for tea, just in time to stop my mother telephoning the police. She thought she had been burgled. My mother came to see the play a lot that week, she felt more at home in the Grand Theatre than she did in her empty house.

GORDON JACKSON
Actor

I was in a very grand, serious medieval piece, with music by Stravinsky, called *The Soldier's Tale*. At one point, I had to stand alone in the middle of the stage, and realise that I had sold my soul to the Devil! Very emotionally, I looked up to Heaven, and cried:

'Now, what am I to do? What do I do now?'

A little boy in the front row cried out, 'Dial 999!!'

I burst out laughing — and, of course, so did the audience! It held up the show for about ten minutes!!

DAVID JACOBS

Broadcaster

MY MOST EMBARRASSING MOMENT

On a cold December night in the mid-70s I was asked to host a beauty competition in a South London cinema. When I arrived I was rather saddened by the lack of beauty and also by the fact that the cinema was without central heating, but I thought that by the time the show started a full house of enthusiastic spectators would warm the place up. Sadly the event inspired only fifty people to attend and they were mostly relatives of the contestants.

There is little doubt that it was one of the dreariest pageants I have ever compèred but, as a true professional, I tried to whip up as much enthusiasm as possible. The twelve contestants paraded in bikinis, their goose-pimples, caused by the cold cinema, doing nothing to enhance their beauty! When the time came and the judges had made their decision I had the unenviable task of calling on the winner and the runners-up in the time-honoured fashion of reverse order. When I announced the third and second there was a mixture of whistles and cheers from the sparse audience, and then came the moment everyone had been waiting for, the winner was to be announced. When I called out her number there were shrieks of derision from the assembled company as on came the plainest girl of all. I looked at her in stunned shock for I had called out number 6 instead of number 9 — my card was upside down!

There was nothing for it but to reveal my mistake, whereupon number 6 howled like a dying cat and number 9 ran on looking, I hasten to add, not all that much prettier, but certainly with the look of victory on her face and the requisite tears of joy for such time-honoured institutions as the crowning of Miss Wherever. Poor old number 6! Poor me! I had to face the wrath of her family and fianceé but that, as they say, is show-business.

SALLY JONES

Presenter

I was interviewing the Irish comedian Dave Allen who assured me beforehand that he would do a straightforward conversation on his life and the differences he had found between Irish and English humour. When it came to the interview he suddenly reversed roles and started to question me about my own life, asked me out very cheekily on air, asked me whether I had a boyfriend — and whether he would get jealous if I went out with Dave. He then insisted on a kiss — and then informed me (on prime-time television!) that he had herpes — luckily he was joking. I blushed and laughed and could hear in my earpiece the show's director saying 'Quick camera 2, go close up on Sally, she's going bright puce!'

It was only when we got off air that Dave confessed he'd been put up to it by my so-called 'friends' in the newsroom. Afterwards we all had a good laugh — and this was the interview that got the most requests for a repeat from viewers!

JOHN JUNKIN
Actor/Writer

Some years ago, I was shopping in a London supermarket, when I realised I was being discussed by two other customers; a small, elderly, red-faced man and his wife. Eventually he came over to me and prodded me with the inevitable forefinger.

'Hey!' he said.

'Yes?' I answered.

'D'you come from Bradford?'

'No.' I assured him.

He returned to his wife for another whispered conversation. Then he returned. Another prod.

'Hey!' he said.

'Yes?' said I, once more.

'D'you drive a tanker?'

'No.'

Once more he returned to his lady for further consultation. Something obviously decided upon, he returned to me.

'Hey!' he said, 'Do you know summat?'

'What?' I asked.

'You've got a ********** double.'

And he walked off.

GORDEN KAYE

Actor

During our Pre-West End tour of the stage play of 'Allo
'Allo!', we were playing in Liverpool and staying at the
famous Adelphi Hotel. Many of the staff are youngsters —
possibly part of a YTS scheme, and on one particular
morning I went down to the dining room and asked the
young waiter for coffee and brown toast. He brought the
coffee straight away, and after about five minutes came
back, and in his inimitable 'Scouse' accent said: 'There
weren't no brown, so I burnt the white!' (and he had).

One could only marvel at the initiative!

CHRIS KELLY
Writer/Producer/Presenter

Since I've done 'Wish You Were Here' on ITV and a programme on BBC Two called 'Food and Drink' I've had many exotic restaurant encounters. I've survived goat in Jamaica and reindeer tongue in Finland but the most alarming entry I've ever seen on a menu was in a small town called Brno in Rumania. First of all I should explain that the lights were very low in this particular eating place, just as they are everywhere in Rumania. After a few minutes conditioning my eyesight to the gloom, I managed at least to make out the fact that one column of the menu was in what appeared to be English translation. I say appeared to be because it featured words that you won't find in any dictionary. It was as though someone had chucked a whole lot of letters up in the air and let them stay where they landed.

Anyway, after a bit I got to the fish section and was chilled to see two words that were familiar, though rarely spotted next to each other. They were 'Steamed Crap.' I think the latter was a misprint for carp but I wouldn't like to swear.

KENNETH KENDALL

Presenter

One evening when reading the News on BBC-TV something dropped with a little 'plop' on the desk in front of me. I paid no attention and went on reading. A short while later when I looked down to turn the page of my script I saw to my horror a whole tooth lying there.

I naturally couldn't start an examination of my mouth in front of the cameras but it wasn't long before I realised that one of my front teeth had fallen out leaving a charming gap, which I tried to cover by reading with a very stiff upper lip. When it was all over a friend asked me if I'd been drinking as I'd started slurring my words. He hadn't seen the real cause of my impaired diction.

The whole incident was hugely embarrassing at the time, but amusing to look back on.

JOHN KETTLEY

Weatherman

A funny incident for me was my wedding day.

I go back to 1981. We chose April because I believed that the worst of the winter's weather was behind us. Not a bit of it!

Heavy snow in the Pennines (the venue) meant that I had to travel 12 miles to the church behind a SNOW PLOUGH. My wife had to leave the hairdresser's because of a power cut. She travelled six miles to an alternative hairdresser's — through the snow.

At the church, she arrived more or less on time in blue wellingtons. And they say it's good luck to get married in the snow.

THE LATE
ROY KINNEAR

Actor

While I was in the army, defending Wales against the Koreans, Morgan, the Battery 'Nutter' came into the office for a 48-hour pass. The Battery Commander agreed to the pass as long as Morgan first got his hair cut and told him that, while he was on his way to the camp barber's he was to drop the Commander's golf clubs off at the Officers' Mess. Just as he got to the Officers' Mess, the Regimental C.O. emerged.

'Ah, Gunner, are you off to play golf?' he asked.

'No, sir, I'm going to get my hair cut.' Morgan replied.

He got seven days confined to barracks for insubordination.

THE KRANKIES
Comedy Team

We're boating people and love nothing better than sailing out to sea to escape the hurly-burly of life on shore. A few years ago we took delivery of a new boat at Bournemouth and decided to take Ian's mom on a sailing trip with us. Trouble is, the boat sprang a leak and we had to beach her just off the shore and paddle to safety. Nothing funny in that, you might say, but the joke came when we reached a secluded beach which was for the exclusive use of nudists. We walked up that beach not knowing which way to look, and Ian's mom had her hands over her eyes. To be honest, the nudists were probably more embarrassed than us and we had fits of giggles about it for ages afterwards.

MAUREEN LIPMAN
Actress

The only remarkable medical thing that happened to me recently was that I told the following favourite joke of mine under full anaesthetic. This apparently takes some doing!

Have you noticed how jokes always come in batches of three? Like comic business in a farce? Or bad news? You hear no jokes for weeks, then somebody tells you three. Apparently, the real comedians seldom laugh when they're told a joke. Like doctors, they nod, say 'Ah, ah' and mentally file it away until they can convince themselves they thought of it in the first place. Almost every ethnic minority has a mythology of jokes on its back, and all is fair, I feel, provided everyone gets lambasted. I once went on

'The Parkinson Show.' Michael, I mean (Mind you, *there's* an idea for an enterprising producer. 'The Cecil Parkinson Show.' 'Live from his constituency, he-e-e-ere's Cecil! And tonight's star guest — Victoria Principal!') Sorry, bad taste. Where was I?

Michael asked me beforehand to tell my favourite joke. It was, and is, the two Jewish ladies discussing their husbands:

Minnie: 'Don't talk to me about my Benny. He makes me sick.'

Bella: 'Why?'

Minnie: 'Because yesterday he brought me home a dozen long-stemmed red roses.'

Bella: 'So what's wrong with that? Very nice he should bring you home roses.'

Minnie: 'You don't know what I have to do when he brings me roses.'

Bella: 'So tell me.'

Minnie: 'Well, *first* I have to go into the bedroom! And *then*, I have to take off all my clothes. And *then*, I have to dance around the bedroom. *Then* I have to lie on the bed. *Then* I have to put my legs in the air.'

Bella: 'You don't have a vase?'

Reproduced by kind permission of Maureen Lipman and Robson Books Ltd from *How Was it for you?*

BARBARA LOTT

Mrs Lumsden in Sorry!

Some years ago, my husband and I had a small cottage deep in the woods, in Sussex; it had been a kennelman's cottage to a large Manor House. To get to it, we had to cross three fields, carrying all our provisions, luggage etc, having left the car at the garage of the big house. If there was a very dry spell a tractor could get down to us. It was during a hot dry spell towards the end of the summer that we ordered the winter coal. Imagine our horror when the following weekend arriving from London, crossing the fields we could see a huge black shape by the back door.

IT WAS THE COAL!!

Unfortunately — the key to the cottage was always kept under two bricks outside the back door, now under half a ton of coal!!

We set to work with shovels, and some hours later, staggered into the cottage, in our best London clothes, coal-black from head to foot. Also among the weekend provisions was a bottle of sherry, most of which we had now drunk.

It was a bad beginning to our weekend, though it makes me smile now.

IAN McCASKILL

Weatherman

When asked for a humorous story for this book Ian
McCaskill replied:
  'I don't know any!'

LEO McKERN

A.O.

Actor/Writer

Gout, toothache, and haemorrhoids have aroused laughter for thousands of years except in those unfortunates with first-hand experience of any of them, but there are some extremely amusing stories about glass eyes and their owners that I tell without embarrassment (so long as I feel the company won't be embarrassed either) and share the enjoyment. One of them, but it is not a joke at all, but on record, concerns an American. Because of a good eye that became increasingly blood-shot in pace with his alcoholic intake at parties, he had a set of glass eyes made whose progressive redness matched his own natural one, changing them as the festivities wore on; his private joke was the last one, which demonstrated his patriotism and feeling of well-being displaying, instead of a pupil, the Stars and Stripes.

And I must say that I have used my 'personal prop' in probably rather shocking and even distasteful ways, absently tapping it with a ball-point at rehearsals, for example; and on one occasion, after a bottle of Chianti with friends in Bertorelli's, half-submerging it in the Spaghetti Bolognese and complaining to the waitress.

I do not justify, or seek excuse for, this kind of behaviour, but offer a possible reason for it: I think it was James Agate who implied that an actor's abilities are broadened by a characteristic 'touch of the gutter.'

Reproduced by kind permission of Leo McKern, A.O., from his book *Just Resting*, published by Methuen, London.

NORRIS McWHIRTER

Author/Editor/Publisher

A COLLISION BETWEEN TWINS

Norris and Ross McWhirter in Malta's Grand Harbour in sister ships (minesweepers).

Up the Red Sea we steamed at ten knots with a tail wind of ten knots astern. The rise in the engine-room temperatures of our steel ship was almost beyond belief. The hardihood of the stokers was quite remarkable and their consumption of water and sugar-coated salt pills was necessarily prodigious. One ship in our flotilla had been visited in Singapore by two of the many new Labour MPs. On reaching the boiler room where the temperature was 160 degrees, they could have been forgiven for turning heel and rushing back because they thought the ship was actually on fire. On the second day under these very trying conditions, Ross and I passed (rather than celebrated) our 21st birthday, since I saw absolutely no point in mentioning the matter any more than one would declare a Silver Wedding anniversary when in jail or announce that one was a preference share holder at a meeting of unsecured creditors. When we got to Suez we had to moor several times to let the larger ships through and to form up a north-bound convoy. I remember swimming across the famously polluted canal and cutting my foot on a metal object. Only the immediate application of the most powerful antiseptics aboard prevented sepsis setting in. At Port Said we received an extraordinary signal which read: 'To *Scaravay* from Flag Officer-in-Charge, Malta. On entering Grand Harbour, Valetta, berth alongside *Shillay*.' I worked out that Ross was now 137 miles away. At 3 p.m. on the afternoon of the 24th August 1946 we entered the Grand Harbour. I was searching for *Shillay* with my binoculars. I spotted her quite close to. Suddenly I was conscious that both the pilot, whom we had picked up outside the harbour, and the Captain, Lieutenant Commander Poynton, were in a per-turbed state. The reversing gear on the main engine had failed and we could not reduce way by going astern which is the only maritime equivalent of applying the brakes.

A fast decision had to be made. Either we should ram the Egyptian Royal Yacht *El Mahroussa* which was in our path, or swing to starboard and strike the *Shillay*. The Captain, with visions of diplomatic ruptures, courts martial and endless paperwork, quickly selected the wiser course. So, accordingly, the unsuspecting *Shillay*, which was having a 'make and mend' after a prolonged spell of dan laying, was clouted so hard that she rocked under the impact. Her crew emerged on the upper deck, and, seeing me, could not understand how their First Lieutenant had got aboard the offending sister ship so quickly. They were totally flummoxed to find identical looking 'jimmys' in the two ships — an identity enhanced by the wearing of identical uniforms. Ross, who had not been expecting us for at least two hours, emerged on the deck looking noticeably thinner in the face and rather strained — the legacy of his very prolonged hours under the cramped conditions in a minor war vessel.

Our collision turned out to be highly popular with the *Shillay* because it gave them four unscheduled days of shore leave while the dockyard 'mateys' worked to replace the buckled plates. The 'Collision and Grounding Report' exonerated us so there were no Court Martials. That evening Ross and I went ashore together for a reunion dinner at Jack's Restaurant. It was a fixed menu but to us the greatest *table d'hôte* we had ever experienced, before or since. It consisted of a whole roast pullet apiece with two fried eggs on a mound of chips and tinned green peas, followed by tinned peaches and cream.

Reproduced by kind permission of Norris McWhirter and Churchill Press, London.

SALLY MAGNUSSON

Presenter

Funny things are always happening in TV studios or out on location. Usually they don't seem quite so funny at the time, but we can get a laugh when the programme is over.

One of my most embarrassing moments was when I was doing a special report about nuclear power 'live' from the Sizewell A nuclear power station. My son was only four months old at the time and I was still breastfeeding him regularly. I left him at home that day, but as the time wore on I became more and more full of milk. I was getting increasingly uncomfortable, but that was the least of the problem. As the cameras rolled for the evening broadcast and the countdown began, I noticed two stains beginning to spread over my clean, beautifully ironed dress. Milk! It was too late to change, too late even to stuff tissues under the offending spot. I had to talk to the nation with milk pouring out of me for all to see.

Fortunately everyone thought it was a great joke. As my husband said, the newspapers next day ought to have carried the headline: LEAK AT SIZEWELL.

ALFRED MARKS

O.B.E.

Actor/Comedian

Walking down the road one day I was approached by a beggar.

'Excuse me mate,' he said, 'can you spare me a fiver for a cup of coffee?'

'A FIVER,' I said, 'a coffee only costs about eighty pence.'

He replied, 'I know ... but I like to leave a big tip.'

DR. PATRICK MOORE

C.B.E.

Astronomer

Way back around 1959, I was presenting a live television programme about astronomy. I opened my mouth to make some world-shattering pronouncement − and in flew a large fly.

What to do?

To my eternal credit, I swallowed it. The producer said afterwards that he saw a look of glazed horror come into my eyes; then I gave a strangled gulp, and went on.

My mother had the answer. 'Yes, dear,' she said thoughtfully. 'Nasty for you, but so much worse for the fly!'

I suppose it was.

MIKE MORRIS

Presenter

I was presenting 'Good Morning Britain' with Anne Diamond one morning and Chris Tarrant (presenter and Capital Radio disc jockey) was a guest.

Unknown to me, Tarrant had a pre-arranged practical joke to play. He held in his hands what I thought was a priceless and very rare Ming dynasty vase. He told me it was virtually unbreakable. To my horror, he started to tap it violently. Suddenly he gave it a firm rap and the vase I thought was a rich treasure fell in fragments all over Chris. The camera zoomed in on my face. Fortunately I kept my mouth shut (a swear word was forming in my brain) and my face just went white as a sheet. I remember thinking that Tarrant had just finished his career. Fortunately I was wrong and the joke and some of the fragments were on me.

BRIAN MURPHY

Actor

It was the Edinburgh Festival 1963. Theatre Workshop under the direction of Joan Littlewood was presenting Shakespeare's *Henry IV Parts I & II*. I was struggling with the two roles of Bardolph and Worcester (one of the wicked uncles).

They were in fact great roles to play, one comic and the other villainous. However, there was often little time between their separate appearances to make the change of costumes and make-up. The Assembly Hall where we were playing was not a conventional theatre and there were long passages and corridors to be negotiated before one reached the stage from one's dressing room. On the first night, still not too familiar with the lay-out of the hall, I left the stage as Bardolph, dashed along a corridor to change my costume into Worcester and set off to return on stage at another point. I pounded up some stairs, through some double doors and emerged into a private sanctum where a gentleman was seated reading a book. He looked totally startled at my strange appearance, clad in a dark cloak with false beard clinging uncertainly to my chin. I apologised and set off again at the double to find the right way. It was then I heard my cue to enter. So, making for the direction of the voices I hurtled along a corridor, threw open some more double doors and breathlessly began to speak my opening lines.

It was then I realised I was surrounded by a very bewildered audience and I was on the *upper balcony*. It was some time before the actors on stage located my voice and we continued the scene shouting at each other to the utter amazement of audience and actors alike.

DEREK NIMMO

Actor/Writer

Over the years I have appeared on television in an assortment of ecclesiastical comedy series. In one year in fact I played an Anglican vicar fourteen times and a Catholic monk seven. Once, memorably, on Christmas Day I played a nun as well — a sight that it was said was nearly enough to make Danny La Rue reach for his trousers.

In my experience, however, the hazards of appearing both in Catholic and Protestant series are, one can only say, manifold.

For instance, I once had to fly to Rome to film a sequence for my 'Oh Brother' series in St. Peter's Square. Whilst the cameras were being set up I wandered away in my monastic robes to inspect the great basilica. En route I met a very charming Englishman who stopped me and asked whether I would mind having my photograph taken with his equally charming daughter. There seemed to be no particular problem involved, so I put one arm . . . or perhaps two . . . around her whilst Pa happily snapped away.

As I started to return to my film unit, I felt an unfriendly hand on my shoulder. When I turned around I discovered that it was attached to the equally unfriendly arm of a Vatican policeman. He indicated that I should accompany him and as his companion was one of those Swiss Guard chaps carrying a very long spike, I decided I had little choice. I was taken across the square and put into a singularly dreary cell somewhere beneath the Curia. It was there that I discovered that I had been 'shopped', I believe the word is, by a nun. Apparently she had decided that by wrapping my arms around a young lady I was not only behaving in a thoroughly unmonkly way but was also most decidedly carrying Christian love too far.

The police demanded to know my identity. I told them that I was an actor, which didn't impress them terribly, and that I was working with the BBC, which seemed to impress them still less. They then went to look for my film crew, but my gallant producer, seeing my arrest, had fled back to the hotel, taking the unit with him. The BBC, he asserted, couldn't get involved.

Unfortunately, the Chief of Police turned out to be an Anglophobe of the first order. It seemed that whilst serving in the Italian army he had been captured by the British in the Western Desert and had then spent the rest of the war working on a potato farm near Wigan. This experience seemed to have soured him against the race in general and me in particular. My trouble was that I had absolutely no way of identifying myself. I was wearing this rather grotty robe (the real monks these days wear lovely silk and mohair outfits), a quick crucifix and some rather ill-chosen rosary beads, whilst on my head rested my BBC-issue pink plastic tonsure, held on by ladies' hair grips. This last mentioned object seemed to offend them most and it was removed from my head and placed on the Police Station table — to act as Exhibit 'A.'

76

As time went by I became even more pompous than usual and demanded to see my consul and/or ambassador, all to no avail. My producer refused to answer the telephone and as they seemed to be getting rather bored with me, they popped me back into my cell.

Some eight hours later a rather timely miracle happened in the shape of an Irish Dominican monk. He had just returned from leave to County Cork, and presumably had spent the whole time locked to his sister's television set, for he was able to account for me. The Chief of Police then turned decidedly more cheery and my release was arranged. They took away my robes, handed me a blanket – and told me not to make a habit of it.

Having made good my getaway from the Eternal City, I flew back to continue filming in England. Within moments of the cameras beginning to turn, I was hit in the face with an ecclesiastical plank. This whacked me hard around the face, removed a couple of teeth and blackened one eye. I was taken to the nearest hospital where the Indian doctor

77

who examined me had only recently arrived from Delhi. He asked me to tell him exactly what happened. I had a go.

'Well, doctor?' I said, as he wrote it all down. 'I was in this church d'you see, standing on a plank balanced on a log in front of the altar.' For some reason he asked me to repeat this. I did.

'And then, doctor, there were these two fat monks standing on top of the altar.'

'Did you say *monks*?' he asked.

'Well, actually, I did, and these two monks jumped off the top of the altar onto the end of the plank in the hope of sending me up ...'

'Sending you up?'

'Yes, that is exactly right, sending me up into the air, so that I could grab hold of the chandelier.'

'What chandelier was that?'

'The one in the church that I intended to swing on, but it didn't work out that way. When the monks jumped, the plank slew round and bashed me, as you can see.'

At this point, curiously enough, the good doctor decided to stop writing.

TOM O'CONNOR

Comedian

I suppose my most peculiar experience was when I was working on *S.S.Canberra*.

One evening I was going to dinner when a little old lady stopped me and said, 'You're that Tom O'Connor off the telly. Can you wait here while I go and get my camera?'

I stood round waiting, trying to straighten my hair when she came back with the camera and said, 'Here you are — you look through here and press the red button!'

IAN OGILVY

Actor

Ten years ago I played Simon Templar in a new version of Leslie Charteris' 'The Saint.' We shot many of the scenes in the streets of London and inevitably collected large crowds who watched the filming with rapt attention. It was quite obvious what we were filming — all our equipment trucks and vans carried the famous 'stick' man logo. One day a small boy come up and tugged me by the sleeve.

'Yes, son?'

''Ere, mister — when's the *real* Roger Moore coming?'

BILL OWEN

M.B.E.

Actor/Author

SCENE

Kate and Bill Owen Saturday morning shopping in the High Street. They are having an argument as they walk along. Kate is trying to persuade her husband as to the merits of cooking by electricity as against gas which they use and Bill prefers.

Kate: Why do you always have to lose your temper whenever we talk about this?

(pause)

Bill: Because we never stop talking about it!

(pause) Are you aware that we started this argument in bed this morning?

(He turns to find he is now talking to a very large policeman)

Policeman: Well I won't say anything if you don't!

(Kate is discovered looking into North East Electricity Showrooms).

P.S. They cook by electricity now.

NICK OWEN

Presenter

I always smile when I think of my hopeless inability at Do-
It-Yourself work. I am always drilling holes in the wrong
place and creating air bricks in our house where they aren't
needed and most of the shelves at home are at a slight angle
which wasn't intended. I always tell my wife Jill they add
character to the place.

One day I had a problem with the car. The door handle
had come off inside and in a fit of courage and inspiration
I decided to have a go at repairing the damage. I was in the
car for about half an hour in a state of increasing frustration
and anger. I managed to take the inside door panel off and
could see exactly what I needed to do. However, there was
a pane of glass in the way and hard as I tried to shift it, it
just wouldn't move. I tried everything to shift it without
breaking it so that I could get at the part of the door to
which I needed to re-attach the inside handle. In
desperation, and having learnt more swear words than I
ever thought had been invented, I went back inside the
house to tell my wife Jill that I was giving up.

'How stupid,' I said, 'the manufacturers are to put a
flaming pane of glass inside the door panel. What is the
point of a pane of glass in such a ridiculous place? And how
on earth are you expected to get at anything the other side
of it?'

'Have you thought of winding up the window?' she asked.

The awful truth dawned. I wound up the window, the
pane of glass was no longer in the way and the job was done
within seconds. I think it is fair to say I am not a born
handyman!

JEREMY PAXMAN

Presenter/Reporter

I well recall being sent out as a young reporter to cover an industrial dispute in Belfast. I found the Trade Union representative, set up the camera, and on the signal, I asked him the first question:

'Mr Kennedy, what's behind this dispute?'

Mr Kennedy was silent. Thinking he hadn't heard me I said again, 'Mr Kennedy, what's this dispute about?'

Silence again. I concluded that he was deaf so I shouted at him, 'Mr Kennedy, what on earth is this dispute about?'

Finally a response.

'The only dispute here is that my name's Johnson and not Kennedy.'

ARTHUR PENTELOW

Mr Wilkes in Emmerdale Farm

I was at a bus stop in the Headrow, Leeds, waiting as usual for the bus that never comes, when I became aware of an old chap next to me, also waiting for the elusive transport. He eyed me up and down with great care and then said, with an economy worthy of the most monosyllabic Yorkshireman, 'Eh, lad, tha's given me an hour or two of pleasure,' and then closed up like a clam. I went to work with a light heart that day.

MAGGIE PHILBIN

Broadcaster

I was travelling in a car with my parents when I was about six years old. Suddenly I piped up from the back seat, 'I know why Whisky (pet dog) hasn't had any puppies.'

My parents froze in anticipation of the answer.

'Because,' I continued, 'we aren't giving her the right kind of dog biscuits!!'

FREDERICK PYNE

Actor

Obviously, because I have been involved with 'Emmerdale' for some time now, there have been lots of hilarious moments which, thank goodness, the viewers haven't seen!

One day though, when I wasn't anywhere near the locations or our studios, something unusual happened. I was at home awaiting the delivery of a new fridge. I heard the sound of a large truck pulling up in my yard and then the doorbell rang. Quickly, I started to prop open doors and make room for the men to carry the fridge into my kitchen. I opened the door, and the man standing there said, 'Hello, Matt, I hope you don't mind me botherin' you, but I thought you might be able to 'elp me.' I was led to his truck to discover that the man had several sheep in the back, which he said weren't eating their food, and was there anything I could do??!! I to this day don't know whether it was a joke or not, but he certainly looked serious enough.

I'd like to think that it was my realistic portrayal of 'Matt Skilbeck' that convinced him I could be of assistance, but it's much more likely that he was a practical joker!!

BERYL REID

Actress

The summer before last, on a very hot day, I had had a few of my great friends to lunch and we had eaten a lot and also had rather a lot to drink. When they all left at about 3.30 in the afternoon, I took all my clothes off and fell asleep on top of the bed. When I woke up there was a printed note through my letterbox saying 'Your Windows have been Cleaned' — and I think this rather got about the village.

ANNEKA RICE

Presenter

The funniest thing that ever happened to me was during a 'Treasure Hunt' in Somerset. I ran up to a grounds man to ask him for a lift in his cart and he agreed to give us a lift if we helped him load his cart with grass cuttings.

I bent down to give him a hand and heard a loud rip. My jump suit had split in a rather embarrassing place and I had to run the next part of the course with a map covering my embarrassment. Graham, my cameraman, taped me up during the commercial break, but the wodge of black tape he used looked worse than the split!

SUE ROBBIE

Presenter

Thinking about my life and its little surprises I've come to realise that a large part of it comprises a whole string of embarrassing moments.

From the time when, as a schoolgirl, I'd arranged to meet my friend Vivian Kerwin in town, saw her, waved, rushed over to greet her ... only to discover at the last minute that I was actually grinning foolishly at my own reflection in a mirrored column outside Marks & Spencer; to the time that, as a teacher performing in a school play, I sat on a chair and promptly fell off the stage, chair and all, to land in an ungainly heap at the feet of 4H.

Now I try to take life more calmly. I adore living in the country and adopting healthy pursuits − riding, walking, cycling. Quite recently my friend's grown-up children called round on their bikes and suggested we all 'take the air' on the towpath by Macclesfield Canal. It was wonderful; perfect weather for early Spring; lots of birdsong, very few people and the first time I'd been out on my bike all year. Occasionally the path would narrow and, feeling responsible, I could hear myself adopting a cautionary parental tone − quite unnecessarily as it turned out. In fact I wish I hadn't, because ... yes − almost inevitable really − suddenly I wobbled, leaned out too far, failed to right myself and, describing a graceless arc, found myself plummetting headlong into the foulest, muddiest stretch of canal you could ever hope to avoid. NOT a pretty sight but those things somehow put life into perspective.

ROBERT ROBINSON

Commentator

I'm not sure whether the word *was* a misprint or not, but in an article about Ivy Compton Burnett I think they *meant* to say the word 'books' when they said 'Her books are as perfect as pieces of music — you couldn't improve them.' What actually got printed was 'Her looks are as perfect as pieces of music — you couldn't improve them.' As I say, it might not be a misprint, but when you recall that Dame Ivy looked like Austen Chamberlain wearing a bird's nest, there is room for doubt ...

Reproduced by kind permission of Robert Robinson from his book *The Dog Chairman.*

JEAN ROGERS

Actress

I am sure many well known TV personalities have 'odd' things said to them. The most common for me, playing Dolly Skilbeck in 'Emmerdale Farm', is 'Oh look, there's Whatshername from Crossroads!' or 'It's so nice to meet you, you're my biggest fan.'

I remember going to a Church fête once with my screen husband Matt, played by Frederick Pyne. We were in our own finery — not our character's clothes — and we sat at a table to sign photos, neatly placed between the potted plant counter and the cake stall. A little old lady was making her way round the exhibits and she paused in front of us, somewhat bemused as to what we were selling. We politely explained, whereupon light dawned and she said apologetically, 'Oh I'm so sorry! It's Matt and Dolly, isn't it? I didn't recognise you with your clothes on!'

REV. ROGER ROYLE
Broadcaster

I was sitting at home one day when the telephone rang and
it was some people asking me if I could possibly get down
to Paignton that evening to speak at a dinner. I replied that
if they could get me there, I would certainly go. They then
made the arrangements for a taxi to pick me up at home,
and take me to Paddington. I caught the train to Newton
Abbot, changed there and caught the little train to
Paignton.

On reaching Paignton there was a gentleman waiting to
greet me, looking very smart indeed in a dinner jacket and
it was very obvious that someone had let them down and
I was standing in at the last minute. I asked the gentleman
'Who am I standing in for?' He replied, 'Diana Dors.' At
that moment I knew there was no way in which I could
possibly win that evening!!

ANDREW SACHS
Actor/Writer

In the days of the late fifties, when real theatrical digs were
not the rarities they are now. I was touring the North of
England and arrived at Mrs Horsley's (name changed to
protect the innocent etc) terrace house where she offered
Bed and Breakfast for two pounds ten shillings a week or
three pounds with evening meal. You may smile but this
was serious money in those days. She ran a somewhat
eccentric household, even for a theatrical landlady. Hurdles
were permanently set up in the long hall-way for her
greyhound to jump over, a spoilt animal that was fed on raw
eggs and had its coat rubbed with brandy – or was it the

other way round? Metal furniture painted with a grain effect to simulate wood graced the front parlour, in which her 20-year-old son lounged for most of the day, limp-eyed, -limbed, and -brained. A demanding lad — 'He keeps us going for shirts alone' Mrs Horsley would complain — his only ambition was to join the police force, but since he had a criminal record, he was presumably destined for a life-time of unemployment. There was above all Mr Horsley, a powerful presence who was never seen, but ruled the house from the back kitchen, from which he grunted loudly in support of whatever Mrs Horsley shouted to him from other parts of the house.

'Oh yes, we've had all the stars here, haven't we, George?'

'Hmph!' from George.

'When was it the Beverley Sisters stayed here?'

Another grunt from the kitchen.

'There you are, what did I tell you?' and so on.

One morning I asked to have a bath — well, it wasn't a matter of course in those days.

'Oh, we don't do baths,' says Mrs Horsley.

'Why not?' I asked politely.

'We don't do baths,' she repeated, 'we haven't done since the war.'

'Well,' I persisted, 'I really will need a bath some time this week.'

'Ay, but we don't do baths.'

I wasn't giving up. 'But Mrs Horsley, you've got a bathroom, with a perfectly good bath in it.'

'Oh ay, perfectly good,'

'Well, why can't I use it?'

'It's George, he doesn't like it,' she raised her voice, 'do you George?'

A predictable grunt from the back kitchen.

She drew me to one side. ''E's funny that way and I wouldn't want to cross him.'

'I don't understand,' I said.

'Well,' she went on, 'George doesn't like other people having baths and I have to say I agree with him, 'cos as he says, with theatricals, you never know who you're following.'

I didn't get a bath that week.

MIKE SCOTT
Presenter

When I was about 22 and searching for a career I became a stage hand with the Festival Ballet for a while (my Dad was a drummer in the orchestra). One matinee I had to go up into the grid high above the stage to drop snow (bits of paper) at the right moment on the Sugar Plum Fairy. The snow was in a bulging bag which I had stuffed inside my shirt while I climbed ladders and walked along catwalks.

I didn't realise two buttons were missing from the shirt! Yes . . . you've guessed!

At the wrong time, two minutes too soon, the bag fell out, missed the principal ballerina by two feet and burst onto the stage. The audience at the Royal Festival Hall collapsed with laughter and I nearly got the sack. Since then I have always checked buttons and zips.

BROUGH SCOTT
Sports Presenter/Journalist

TWO BEAUTIES AND THE BEAST ON THE HILL

12th February 1978
The big freeze has shivered all horse racing to a halt, and every eager racing man is kicking himself for not having fixed up a trip to Cagnes-sur-Mer, in the South of France. That's where we went ten years ago, and a couple of different moves one starry Riviera night could have changed one of jump racing's most famous records, and might even have led me to an examination of France's esteemed prison system — from the inside.

Now I have got nothing against the Hippodrome de la Côte d'Azur. With the blue of the Mediterranean in front of you and the snow-capped peaks of the Alpes Maritimes up behind, it is one of the most beautiful, as well as the most efficient, racecourses in the world. It is just that even the Entente Cordiale can be messed up if you fail to hold your liquor or learn the lingo. On that occasion our team, who were down there because of the foot-and-mouth outbreak in England, had not been unsuccessful. David Nicholson had won the Prix de Bouif on Cavalry Charge and, at six foot in his tights, had been dubbed Le Plus Grand Jockey du Monde, and Irish champion Bobby Coonan had been the first to secure a close personal relationship with a young French lady.

So that Saturday evening Stan Mellor and I were aiming to help things along, he because of his natural charm and I to avoid the attentions of one disgruntled and extremely dusky French punter who had lost his money on me that afternoon.

We seemed to have made a particular friend of a snappily dressed little jockey who never rode very much but was a dab hand with the champagne bottle. Our friend appeared to be insisting that we accompany him and another jockey to a special dinner that night. The restaurant was set high up in the hills, with all the lights of Nice bobbing below, and it was only after we had been taken to the place of honour among some three hundred guests that we noticed something odd about the lay-out. The whole place was built around and above a little sandy square which looked exactly like the stock Mexican setting for a TV western. Our hosts continued to lavish such hospitality on us that we suspected no problems and when, after the fifteenth course and twenty-fifth glass we were asked to go down to the square for *les photographes*, we dismissed the knowing smiles of our fellow guests as a salute to dear old Britannia. But suddenly our friend had disappeared, the door of the courtyard opened and there stood an almighty behorned beast breathing fire and brimstone and apparently holding us responsible for all the wrongs done to the bovine species down the ages.

They said afterwards it was only a heifer, but when the beast all but changed Stan Mellor's epitaph from The First

Man to Ride a Thousand Winners to The First Jockey to Die in the Bullring, and then hit the wooden post next to me with a splintering crash, it was time to take evasive action. With his champion jockey's reactions, Stan found the way first and on my desk today I still have a photo of the intrepid Mellor shinned up a tree with a thin-faced B. Scott grinning drunkenly beside him. There is also another photo of us, riding a donkey, and here's the twist. Our two friends are also in the picture, and are all too clearly identifiable as two of the gang who a few years later served prison sentences for their part in France's most notorious 'fixed' race, the Prix Bride Abattue, and our champagne-opener was proved to be a hit man for the Mafia.

From *On and Off the Rails*, Victor Gollancz Ltd.

SIR HARRY SECOMBE
C.B.E.
Entertainer

A NIGHT IN A CELL

Ever tasted a mug of cocoa made on a gas ring in a police station? What is more, have you ever spent a night in a cell? Well I have. (Pause for excited whispers and shuffling of feet.)

It happened quite a few years ago when I was living in digs in North London. It was an old Victorian house with pillars and wrought iron outside, and on the inside cavernous brown varnished passages full of echoes and with a multitude of landings.

When I first established myself there, I took a first-floor bedroom with breakfast at thirty-five shillings a week, then as my fortunes dwindled I began to rise a floor at a time to less capacious and cheaper rooms. The extent of my success at the time can be judged by the fact that I was now on the top floor in a room which also served as a store for the house-cleaning equipment.

It was the day after Boxing Day and the house was empty except for myself and the housekeeper, the other boarders having gone home until after the New Year. The reason I had stayed on was because I had a cabaret engagement that evening at an hotel in Pinner, for which I was to receive the astounding sum of ten pounds in cash.

The contract had stipulated evening dress, and not being in possession of one, I had hired a dinner suit from a theatrical dress agency. It was not a wonderful fit, and the lapels had a patina of fine grease which shone brightly in the spotlight as I stood in the centre of the floor of the hotel dining-room. The audience was very unappreciative and viewed me with eyes jaundiced by Christmas and Boxing Day excesses. Even the decorations hung limply from the ceiling and my air of desperate gaiety had as much effect on them as the paper hats they wore shamefacedly on their aching heads.

I finished my act in a blaze of indifference and went immediately to the manager for my money.

'Here's your cheque,' he begrudged.

'Can't I have cash?' I said, having only three shillings in my pocket.

'I haven't got authority to cash cheques,' he said grandly and, handing it to me, he walked into his office, shutting the door.

The walk to the tube station was a long one, and a slight drizzle did not help to raise my spirits. I could feel the water beginning to seep through the thin soles of my hired patent dress shoes, and by the time I reeached the digs a full hour later I was thoroughly fed up.

It was now half past one in the morning and as I stood fumbling for my key on the doorstep even the hard bed amongst the brooms seemed enticing. I searched every pocket of the dinner suit but found nothing except the cheque. There was only one thing to do, ring the bell. This was a vain hope, I knew, because the housekeeper lived at the back of the house and was as deaf as a post. I thumbed the bell angrily, the sound echoing uselessly down the dark passageway. Five minutes later, when the battery began to fade, I stopped and began to eye up the pillars speculatively. Above the portico was a window which might be open, if I could reach it.

I had just got to the top of the pillar when a light shone in my face. A policeman's voice from below called 'Hello! Hello! What are you doing up there then?'

I waved fatuously with one hand and slid down again.

'Trying to get in,' I said. 'I've lost my door key.'

'Blimey, it's Raffles!!' said the copper in a heavily jocular

tone, seeing my dinner jacket under the raincoat.

'Can you prove you live here? Got any identification on you?'

Of course I hadn't, only a cheque which was made out to 'Cash' and did not have my name on it. After a few more questions for which I had no reasonable answers, such as what was the housekeeper's name − 'Muriel Something' was not enough − he decided we should go along to the station.

As we walked up the street, the stealthy pad of my rain-ruined shoes sounded sinister against the honest ring of the constable's boots. Already I began to feel guilty and my stammering explanations about being a comedian didn't seem true even to me. When we reached the station the policeman took me straight to the desk sergeant who had his back to us. He turned as the constable declared with an air of triumph, 'We've got a real comedian here, says he is anyway. Caught him trying to break into a house down the road.'

The sergeant gave me a hard look.

'What's your name?' he said. I told him and then still looking at me searchingly, he said, 'Just a minute, weren't you at the Metropolitan Theatre Edgware Road about a month ago in variety?'

'Yes,' I said hopefully.

'This is him, Jack,' he said delightedly to the police constable. 'Remember I told you about the feller doing a shaving act, with the lather all over the place, and then singing at the finish? Well − this is the bloke, Just a sec, I've still got the programme here somewhere.' And rummaging in his desk he produced it. 'Here you are − Harry Secombe, the crazy comedian.'

I breathed a big sigh of relief and launched into a couple of top 'Cs' to clinch the subject of identification. Wincing slightly the sergeant got down to details with the constable and myself and we sorted things out to our mutual satisfaction. 'You might as well stay here the night,' said the sergeant.

'Here's a couple of blankets − take this mug of cocoa and nip down to one of the cells.'

So it was that I spent the night comfortably warmed by Government provided cocoa, lying on a cell cot.

The following morning I bade my uniformed friends a fond farewell and arrived at my chambers in time to catch the housekeeper taking in the milk. She looked at my evening dress.

'Where have you been?' she said archly, hoping to hear of some romantic assignation.

'In jail,' I said.

She laughed, disappointed. 'You theatricals are all the same,' she said, 'always joking.'

'By the way,' I said 'what *is* your last name?'

Raffles,' she said, 'Muriel Raffles.'

Reproduced from *Goon For Lunch*, by kind permission of Sir Harry Secombe and Michael Joseph Ltd.

DINAH SHERIDAN

Actress

We have the 'Bishop of Gibraltar in Europe' next door and he was anxious for me to open an International Christian Bazaar for him. I went round to talk about it, and — as the actress said to the Bishop — we settled the date. Bishop John, unfortunately, would be away, so I was rather holding the fort by myself and not a little nervous. However it must have gone well as I had a visit from Bishop John on his return. He stood at the door with something in his hand which he said was a thank you present for me, he was so grateful and had heard how well it had been received. The present turned out to be a bottle of gin, with a label stuck to it stamped with the beautiful seal of the Bishopric, and in his own handwriting down each said it side: Diocesan Holy Water ...! The actress was very grateful to the Bishop!

ALASTAIR STEWART

Newscaster

In June last year I worked on the General Election which involved starting at 9 p.m. and finishing some time the following afternoon. That involved two hours sleep at about 5 a.m., a change of clothes and a fresh start at 7 a.m.

Unfortunately some helpful colleague, in tidying up my change of clothes, removed my shoes and socks.

Therefore I presented the General Election coverage on day two in a suit, shirt and tie but nothing on my feet. I fear this added to the atmosphere in the studio in a somewhat unpleasant way!

WILLIAM G. STEWART

Presenter/Producer

Many years ago, when I was a young man, and had just started in television with the BBC, I was an assistant on a film-magazine programme on which Richard Burton was appearing. The producer's strict instructions to me were that, any time that Richard Burton was not required, I should escort him from the studio, on the fourth floor at Lime Grove Studios, to the hospitality room on the ground floor.

In those days Richard liked a drink and, in the course of the afternoon and evening, I took him up and down in the lift at least twenty times. By the time the programme was over we had become almost friends. He had asked me about how I started in television, what my ambitions were, my family — all that sort of thing.

At that time the BBC required junior assistants like myself to wear suits and be properly turned out — even though my basic pay at that time was £9.12s 6d a week!

On our last trip down I noticed him discreetly put his hand into his pocket and, from quite a hefty roll, peel off two or three £5 notes. It took me all of three seconds to work out that I was about to get a tip equal to 1½ times my weekly pay. But as the lift doors opened he turned to the uniformed lift-man, and slipped the money discreetly into his hand with the words, 'Thank you for looking after us Charley'. As I followed him out of the lift his words to me were 'Good night Bill, I've no doubt we'll bump into each other again.'

ALAN TITCHMARSH

GardeningExpert/Presenter

I had just finished a 'Breakfast Time' programme. Full of enthusiasm I'd been going on about how good manure was for the garden. I had a bucket of the stuff in front of me on the glass-topped coffee table. Now any gardener will tell you that it's very difficult to keep your hands out of a bucket of manure — you've simply got to give it a squeeze and a crumble to prove to yourself how good it is.

So it was that the programme finished with me up to my elbows in muck as a voice from the other side of the studio rang out: 'Don't shake hands with him; you've seen where they've been.'

I looked up in time to see the Princess of Wales coming towards me with her hand outstretched. We met with a gentle squidge, and all I could think of to say was 'I'll never wash again!'

I hope *she* did.

BARRY TOOK
TV/RadioWriter/Performer

I chair the 'News Quiz' and am known for my occasional stumbles or as Richard Ingrams puts it, 'Took's speech impediment'.

One evening I protested about this, as I saw it, slander, and managed to say 'I don't suffer from any peach impediment.'

CAROL VORDERMAN
Presenter/Writer

One day we were recording 'Countdown' in the Yorkshire Television studios in Leeds and on that day Ned Sherrin was the guest celebrity in Dictionary Corner. As we were walking out of the studio at the end of one of the programmes I started chatting to Ned about *Ziegfeld* which had recently opened in the West End. I was going on about the disappointing reviews and how unkind the critics had been to the show.

Ned turned to me and said 'Well it will be interesting to see what Tommy Steele does to the production' (Tommy Steele had just been brought in as the Director). I said 'Yes, he certainly can't do any worse than they've done already. By the way Ned, have you seen it yet?' Ned turned to me with his 6'3" frame, looked me straight in the eye and said 'Yes darling, I wrote it.'

GEOFFREY WHEELER

Producer/Presenter

My wife and I were returning from holiday in Switzerland. The service on board the British Airways aircraft was nothing short of brilliant and every little request or enquiry I made was dealt with instantly. As we left the aircraft I said to the Chief Stewardess, 'Thank you very, very much indeed you have been so kind and made our flight a real pleasure.'

'Not at all,' she replied. 'It's been a delight to have you on board Mr Baker!'

(For some reason I do seem to get mistaken for Richard Baker every now and again.)

JUNE WHITFIELD

O.B.E.

Actress

This incident happened to an actor in the days when there were lots of touring companies and landladies of the theatrical 'digs' usually saw the show on the Monday night.

This actor checked into his digs on Sunday. The landlady saw the show on Monday and the actor was playing 'Dracula.' After the show he returned to his digs to find the door locked and he had no key. He rang the bell a couple of times and finally the window opened and the landlady looked out. 'I'm sorry,' he said, 'could you let me in?'

'No fear,' said the landlady.

'But I must get in − my things are in there,' he said.

'Not likely,' said the landlady, 'I saw the show − you couldn't do it if you didn't have it in you!'

ROGER WHITTAKER

Singer/Entertainer/Songwriter

After an energetic afternoon playing squash, while on tour in France, I returned to my hotel and dived straight into the shower. Squeaky clean and refreshed I turned off the taps and grabbed a towel. A rustling noise from the bedroom made me pause. I peered around the door of the bathroom, for in spite of the 'Do Not Disturb' signs I invariably hang outside my door, hotel maids religiously ignore these requests for privacy. I did not want to prance out of the bathroom and surprise one of them. The surprise, however, was on me. There on the bed, making herself at home, plumping up the pillows, was a not very attractive, but very naked lady.

Quietly, I closed the door and turned the shower taps back on again while I considered my next course of action. I had it! Natalie! She'd know what to do! Poor Nats, I knew I was asking a lot of her but silently I picked up the telephone handset in the bathroom, hoping to hell the sound of the shower would drown out my conversation, and I dialled home.

I was not warmly greeted. A decidedly distraught Natalie answered the 'phone, her voice the jagged edge of a rusty tin can. In the background I could hear the unmistakeable screeching of a child in the throes of rebellion. In this case, I was told icily, our Emily, aged ten months, was in the process of redecorating herself, Natalie and the kitchen with her afternoon feed.

'Well, speak up!' Natalie shouted down the 'phone, trying to provide a counterpoint to Emily's howling.

'I can't,' I whispered.

'Oh, no, don't tell me you've lost your voice. I'd better call Irene and tell her to cancel tonight's show.'

'No, it's not that,' I said. 'There's a naked woman in my bed.' I felt just as foolish saying it, believe me, as it reads.

'So, what am I supposed to do about that?' said my wife, not sounding as perturbed as I thought a wife ought to be

101

in such circumstances. 'Do you know who she is?' came the next question. Ah, curiosity at least!

'Yes. She's the wife of one of the guys in the hotel,' I replied.

'Well in that case the answer's simple. Call down to the desk and have her removed, but don't bother me with your problems!'

Hmm, most unsympathetic, I thought. But as our conversation was obviously at an end, I hung up and sat down on the edge of the tub, mulling over the problem.

Natalie was right, of course. The thing to do was to have her removed. However, the question was how to do it without getting myself caught in the middle of a husband and wife battle. Would he believe I was just an innocent party? Would she drop me in it to protect her virtue? I sat there so long the lady must have thought I'd disappeared down the plug hole, what with all the water running. Fortunately, she never ventured into the bathroom to investigate the longest running shower in the world, giving me time to find a solution. And suddenly at that point it dawned! I would pretend I didn't know who she was. I grabbed the 'phone and dialled the front desk.

'Sorry to bother you,' I said, 'but I'm faced with a delicate problem. I've just finished my bath and discovered that a lady has obviously mistaken my room for hers and has in fact gone to sleep in my bed. I wonder if a maid could quietly wake her and save the lady embarrassment. I'll remain in the bathroom until this is done.'

I could almost hear the man wink as he said,

'Of course, sir, I'll see to it immediately!'

The shower was still running, I put my ear to the door and a few moments later was rewarded with the sound of voices coming from the bedroom. Then came the sound of the room door closing and, with a sigh of relief, I closed down Victoria Falls and emerged from my hiding place. Natalie and I had a good laugh about it when I got home.

Reproduced by kind permission of Roger Whittaker from his autobiography SO FAR, SO GOOD, published by Columbus Books 1986 copyright control.

DESMOND WILCOX

Writer/Presenter/Producer

I speak as a man passionately devoted to the belief that it is only older women who can fill our hearts and imaginations. Now, before legions of Amazonian young beauties (firm of flesh, clear of eye, white of tooth, long of leg and all of that) descend to tear me apart, let me quickly point out that younger women are, of course, the fresh new springtime of our world. They represent sweetness, promise, challenge. For me that has always been disaster.

I have always loved older women and I have always made a fool of myself over younger ones. Older women know that men aren't Tarzans, that men do get tired, or drunk, or sometimes shed a tear. But in the presence of younger women I tend to become Monsieur Hulot, Norman Wisdom, Danny Kaye — not James Bond or Simon Templar, but Clouseau; not a hero but a clown. I am also convinced that there is something about women as they get older that makes them infinitely more desirable as companions, wives and lovers. The great beauties of our noisy age, who have quickened a million pulses in the breathy darkness of the Odeon or caught our eyes — and even stirred our loins — in the pages of magazines and newspapers, have all, almost without exception, improved with age, like, dare I say, furniture, wine and well-polished shoes?

Prove it? Very well, I will: Joan Collins, Jane Fonda, Sophia Loren. Look at them, then — and look at them, now. They were all sensational beauties in their younger days, it's true, but these aren't just cases of beauty still being there, somehow lingering on. They have improved, grown more attractive, even more desirable as they've grown older. Today these women — at an age when most wealthy wives and mothers are secure in twin-sets, tweeds, pearls and the station wagon rota for picking up the kids from school — are more than ever symbols of allure, mysterious and thought-provoking. Somehow you also know that they are nicer women to know now — and more fun.

Not that sex appeal is a thing of the past for any of them. After all, nobody asked Joan Collins to star in the more explicit movies when she was a younger woman, and they're not asking younger women to do it now. It's Joan Collins they want — because the men and women watching the movie want her. I would suggest that it's also because nobody can fail to see that Joan Collins now enjoys life more than ever and that emotion is bound to transmit to the onlooker. Add maturity and a sense of fun to beauty, put looks with experience — and you're bound to win. For me it's with young women that I've always been doomed to lose.

Even in the days when I courted my wife I still hadn't learned that particular lesson and, at nearly 40, I really should have. I remember finding that we'd been locked out of a car park after dinner in a restaurant. 'Shall we ring the bell for the attendant?' murmured the woman I fancied deeply and wished to impress greatly. But not for me the path of common sense or the way of a helpful suggestion.

'Leave it to me. I'll jump the gate and go down the ramp and bring the car up. I'll be able to unbolt the gate from the other side,' I said in my crispest, chest-beating manner.

'It is rather a high iron gate. Are you sure you can . . .' she started to reply. That did it. I took two steps back in the darkness to the edge of the pavement, nodded firmly for her to step aside, skipped lithely to the gate, placed one hand on the top bar and vaulted into the air . . . I hit the chain-link fencing and crossbar at about 25 miles an hour, travelling horizontally, four feet above the ground — well short of clearing it. My ankle struck the iron upright a mighty blow and my trouser leg ripped from crutch to turn-up as I slumped to the pavement with a most unmanly, only half-strangled, scream. I still have the scar and I've never forgotten the lesson. Well, nearly never.

There was the time when I offered a young woman a lift home from a party and we discovered a car thief trying to break into my parked car. In a trice, I turned into the Clint Eastwood of Chelsea. I clasped both hands together above my head in the lethal position of a karate 'special,' ran quickly forward and brought my hands (deadly weapons that they had become) down from the top of a leap in the air — sufficiently hard to break the strongest man's neck.

But the strong — young — man had taken off while I was still going up in my slow-motion jump. By the time I came down he was 50 yards up the road, running hard. I ran after him, pounding feet, pumping heart, gasping lungs. He gained about three yards in every ten and by the corner of the road he was so far ahead he might as well have been in Slough. I stopped and stumbled back to the young, and concerned, lady. From admiring fan she became heroine nurse, which was just as well. I went into hospital the next day with a severe rupture.

'What the devil have you been up to at your age?' murmured the surgeon, as he prepared me for the anaesthetic, the knife — and the scar that has since ruined my bikini-wearing holidays.

But I still can't resist the challenge to prove myself in the eyes of younger women. Once, in Jamaica, I nearly drowned, shipwrecked on my sailboard and lacerated by a coral reef, because I thought all the good-looking young women on the beach would think much less of me if I called 'Help!' Once I managed to keep smiling with half a ton of horse standing quite still on my crushed big toe, because I just didn't want to admit to the young stable girl that an expert like me had forgotten the basic rules of horse handling. Once I stepped backwards off a boat while didactically lecturing two young ladies on the dangers and risks of life at sea. And once I dived into a river to save a young girl who'd fallen in, only to find, as I reached her, that she was standing on the bottom.

By now I should have got the message, understood the problem that my machismo over-reacts in the presence of attractive young women. I know it, but my damn hormones don't seem to understand. They let me down every time.

Extract reproduced from an article by kind permission of Desmond Wilcox and British Airways *High Life* magazine.

FRANK WILLIAMS

Actor

I began my career in the theatre as an A.S.M., Assistant Stage Manager, in those days an exalted title for one of the lowliest forms of life. In the theatre where I worked, my duties encompassed everything from sweeping the stage and making tea for the members of the cast during rehearsals to prompting and working the sound system during performances. This sound system was primitive even by the standards of its own day — no tape decks or long-playing records in those days, just two old fashioned turntables on which we placed the old 78 r.p.m. recordings. It was used to provide music while the audience came into the theatre and during the intervals, and also to provide the sound effects needed in a play. We had various sets of records with items like car braking, lorry stopping, distant thunderstorm and so on. It was this primitive sound system which was to prove to be my undoing on one famous occasion.

As a theatre we tended to go in for rather elaborate costume plays with grand historical themes and large casts. It was in one of these that a character had the line, 'Hark, I hear a distant trumpet.' I looked through our effects records, cars, lorries, horses and even church bells in plenty but no trumpets, distant or otherwise. I consulted with the senior stage manager. They had obviously met this problem before. He produced a recording of the Leonora Overture on which had been marked with a crayon a yellow circle, and instructed me at the appropriate moment to place the needle on the yellow circle and one would get the solo trumpet call. All went well for several performances. I was playing a part in the play as well as all my other duties, and came the fatal day when I was having a little trouble with my beard. I was in the dressing room re-sticking it when I realised the distant trumpet line was getting perilously near. I rushed to the sound corner just in time, placed the record on the turntable and the needle on the yellow line — as I thought. But in my flustered state, I must have missed, for as the actress said 'Hark I hear a distant trumpet,' there were several loud and crashing chords from the entire Halle orchestra.

It was rather a heavy play, and the audience seemed to enjoy it — it gave them the only real laugh of the evening. The actress playing the scene spoke to me again eventually, and the sound system and I became quite friendly; except that is for the other occasion when it decided to have a go at me. We used to play the National Anthem at all performances and we had a record 'The National Anthems of the Nations'. I think I was having another bit of bother with a beard when the time for the National Anthem came, but I got there in time and grabbed the record and out came 'The Marseillaise.' It didn't really matter, the audience just looked round to see where the French Ambassador was sitting.

SIMON WILLIAMS

Actor

A woman on a train once said to me, 'I suppose you think you look like that Simon Williams off the telly.'

I said, 'Yes, I suppose I do a bit.'

'Well you don't — he's not so conceited!'

WINCEY WILLIS

Presenter

Setting: Wincey working in Tunisia as a travel courier, escorting holiday-makers on a camel ride led by Ahmed, the Arabian camel-handler.

The camels didn't really need a handler: they didn't have to be told what to do and in fact they had done the trip so often they seemed to be doing it in their sleep. On one occasion we stopped at the camel staging post by the oasis and the camels dropped down on to their knees as usual. One of the tourists was a particularly large lady from Blackpool. She was a really jolly soul, who got into the spirit of everything and even had on her Lawrence of Arabia clothes. I don't know how the camel managed, because she was absolutely enormous. Normally these white robes would be flowing and billowing everywhere, in the hot desert breeze, but on this woman they were stretched taut around her huge body. When she reached the oasis there wasn't really any space left and as the camel ducked down on to its front legs she let out one almighty scream, at the same time propelling her top set of false teeth out of her mouth and down on to the sand. With exquisite timing the camel's rump landed two seconds later and embedded the teeth in the desert.

Trying to explain to Ahmed Ben Ali whatever that he had to get the camel up again, because it was sitting on Ethel's teeth, was one of the hardest things I have ever had to do in a foreign language. He spoke very little French. I spoke very little Arabic. We communicated mainly by sign language and the language that all Arabs seem to understand — money. It was hysterical with me trying to explain that the camel was sitting on Ethel's false teeth and Ethel totally distraught. She couldn't bear the thought of spending the rest of her holiday minus her top choppers and, of course, the rest of the coach party were keeling over on the ground with hysterics.

No one could speak. The tears were rolling down our

cheeks. Eventually Ahmed Ben Ali what's his name kicked the camel several times, until it begrudgingly moved forward a bit, so that three of us could start digging down into the sand. Remarkably, we did find Ethel's teeth. As they had landed on the soft sand they were quite unimpaired, although I'll never know how she could have put them back into her mouth, after they had been under that camel's bum.

Reproduced by kind permission of Wincey Willis, from her book of similar humorous incidents and adventures which she has experienced, *It's Raining Cats & Dogs*, published by Elm Tree Books Ltd.

Bob Wilson

Sports Presenter

Once while presenting a programme called 'Today's Sport,' I had introduced an item on a horse race. I was then told by my editor that when the recording of the race had finished I would be left with just five seconds in which to remind viewers of that evening's 'Match of the Day' programme at 10 p.m. Five seconds isn't much time in which to give that message and say 'goodbye.' In the short time I had to think of the words to use, I thought I might say 'Don't forget "Match of the Day" tonight' or even 'Don't miss "Match of the Day" tonight.' When it came to the moment of truth this is what came out: 'That's all we have time for, but there's "Match of the Day" tonight at 10 o'clock. DON'T FORGET TO MISS IT!!!'

Ernie Wise

O.B.E.

Comedian

I was flying to Las Palmas and was invited up to the cockpit. I said to the pilot, 'How long before we reach Las Palmas?'

He said, 'Oh,' and turned the plane.

He was heading for Tenerife.

TERRY WOGAN

Broadcaster and chat show host

I well remember Monday 18th February 1985 — it was the first evening of the new thrice-weekly 'Wogan' which comes live from the BBC Televison Theatre at Shepherds Bush.

One of my guests was Elton John. I left my chair to walk over to greet Elton who was standing by the piano, went up to shake hands, tripped, not very elegantly, and ended up on the floor with Elton trying to bring me to my feet. After several jolly japes from Elton I regained my composure (I think) and we carried on with the show.

Not a very auspicious start to a new series, but it certainly made the papers the next day, and, much to my mortification guests still come on to 'Wogan' to remind me of that first evening which still brings a flush to the old cheeks!

JIMMY YOUNG
O.B.E.

Broadcaster

An agent sent me to audition for the BBC back in 1949 and received a letter back which said: 'We regret to inform you we feel that Mr Jimmy Young has NO FUTURE IN BROADCASTING.'

They were probably right.